The Private Record: How to Build Lawful Evidence of Truth and Standing

Sovereign Action, Volume 3

Roger Davies

Published by TWON Publications, 2025.

THE PRIVATE RECORD: HOW TO BUILD LAWFUL EVIDENCE OF TRUTH AND STANDING

First edition. October 5, 2025.

ISBN: 979-8232102630

Written by Roger Davies.

Table of Contents

Dedication

For every man and woman who values truth more than argument.

This book is written for educational and philosophical reflection only. It offers no legal or financial advice and encourages all readers to act peacefully and responsibly in life and correspondence.

"The written word is the breath of conscience made visible. Where truth is recorded, silence becomes proof, and peace becomes law."

— Roger Davies

Introduction:
The Record That Speaks for You

Every system that governs the world depends on record. Every transaction, every law, and every judgment rests upon paper that tells story. Governments, councils, and corporations record everything because record transforms assumption into authority. What is written becomes what is remembered, and what is remembered becomes what is believed. The one who keeps record holds truth.

For centuries, record has been foundation of law. In early times, a man's word was his bond, spoken before witnesses. As life grew complex, memory could no longer hold every agreement. Writing replaced speech as proof. The document became living witness that did not forget. From this simple truth, the modern world was built. The living being who understands this gains same power that institutions have used for generations.

The private record is the tool of freedom. It is the written evidence of truth that stands when words are forgotten. It proves honour, intention, and peace. Councils and governments depend on paperwork to justify authority. The Sovereign learns to use paperwork to protect honour. The system fears only one thing, the man or woman who keeps better record than it does.

To build lawful record, you must first value truth more than opinion. The record does not serve pride. It serves clarity. Each letter, notice, and affidavit is act of responsibility. The private record is mirror of conscience. It does not lie because it is created in peace. It speaks for you when you are silent. It remembers when you have moved on. It carries your words beyond argument into permanence.

The man who acts without record is vulnerable to misunderstanding. The man who acts with record is unshakable. Councils can ignore requests, courts can issue orders, and agencies can threaten action, yet they cannot erase what has been written in honour. Paper becomes witness that cannot be intimidated. It tells story of truth calmly and without anger.

Many believe that record belongs only to offices and professionals. This belief is false. Record is natural extension of memory, and every man or woman has right to remember their truth. When you write letter, date it, and keep copy, you are already building lawful record. When you send notice by recorded delivery, you have created chain of evidence stronger than assumption. Law respects those who respect themselves enough to record their words.

The private record differs from public record. Public record serves system. It exists to maintain control and continuity of government. Private record serves conscience. It exists to preserve truth of living being. When the two conflict, private record stands higher because it comes from life itself. The one who keeps accurate and peaceful record cannot be ruled by assumption.

The record does not need approval from council or court. Its authority arises from truth, not permission. Once truth is written, dated, and witnessed, it becomes evidence. No official stamp can add to or remove from it. The value of record lies in the honesty of its author. When you write in peace and good faith, you create document that holds its own power.

To understand record, look at how system uses it. Councils send notices, summonses, and reminders. They always write because writing binds the receiver. The paper is offer that seeks response. If you reply calmly, asking questions and keeping proof of delivery, you join the conversation as equal. If you remain silent, the paper becomes record of your consent. The difference lies not in law but in communication.

Building private record is act of honour because it replaces fear with order. Fear thrives in confusion. Record creates clarity. When you keep copies of letters, date each page, and file everything properly, you no longer fear correspondence. Each envelope becomes entry in your archive of peace. You respond not with emotion but with knowledge. The archive grows, and with it, your confidence.

The private record is not weapon. It is shield. It protects without attacking. It exists so that truth cannot be twisted by misunderstanding. When dispute arises, record provides proof of what was said, when, and by whom. It removes need for memory to fight emotion. The paper speaks calmly in your place. This is why councils fear correspondence that is structured, dated, and delivered with receipt. They cannot argue with their own silence.

Your private record should always reflect who you are. Write clearly. Use full name as living man or woman. Sign each page in blue ink to show life and presence. Store documents neatly in folders. Label everything by date and subject. Keep record both on paper and digitally. Discipline in order mirrors discipline in thought. The more precise your record, the stronger your standing.

Honourable communication does not mean excessive writing. It means deliberate writing. Every letter must have purpose. Each word carries weight. The one who writes too much risks confusion. The one who writes with clarity commands attention. Law follows those who write with intention.

You will discover that as you build record, your view of authority changes. You begin to see councils and agencies not as powerful entities but as collections of clerks responding to letters. Their strength lies in volume, not virtue. They win because people forget to write. When you remember to write and to keep record, balance returns. You meet them on their own ground, and they find themselves without advantage.

The private record also teaches patience. Once notice is sent, you must wait. Time itself is part of process. Silence becomes proof of consent or refusal to answer. Each passing day strengthens your evidence. Many lose power by reacting too quickly. The wise keep still, allowing truth to mature like seed in soil.

This book will show how to create, store, and preserve lawful record. It will explain principles behind notices, affidavits, and declarations. It will teach how to index your documents, manage your correspondence, and use patience as strength. It will not tell you what to believe but will remind you how to prove what you already know to be true.

You will learn how to speak through writing, how to close matters peacefully, and how to stand as living being whose truth is recorded in honour. You will see that every envelope sent and every page signed is act of peace, not protest. You will realise that record keeping is spiritual as much as practical. It disciplines mind and brings order to life.

The private record will outlive you. When created in honour, it becomes archive of conscience for those who follow. It tells future generations that there were men and women who lived by truth rather than fear. It shows that law can exist without force, guided by written word of peace.

In a world ruled by assumption, the written truth of living being becomes light that cannot be extinguished. The system may ignore it, but silence does not erase it. The record remains, patient and powerful, waiting for time to reveal its strength.

You are the keeper of your own truth. You are author of your own record. When written in peace, your word becomes law of your life. That is the essence of sovereignty. That is the purpose of this book.

Chapter 1:
The Law of Record and Memory

Law begins with memory. Before paper, before writing, and before printed law books, men and women lived by spoken word. They remembered promises and repeated them aloud before witnesses. The word carried power because it came from life. The promise spoken truthfully was considered sacred. To break it was to dishonour oneself before the community. In that time, law and conscience were one.

As societies grew, memory alone could not hold the weight of agreement. People needed way to preserve truth beyond the reach of forgetfulness. Writing was born to protect memory from time. A man could carve his word into stone or mark it upon parchment so that his promise would survive him. Thus, record replaced memory as foundation of law.

The principle has never changed. Every court, council, and government today relies on same rule. What is not recorded is presumed not to exist. What is written, dated, and signed becomes fact until proven false. The written word outlives witness and silence alike. The system knows this and uses it to control. The Sovereign learns the same lesson to remain free.

Record is memory made permanent. It is the bridge between mind and law. When you write, you move truth from thought into world of form. Once written, it cannot be easily denied. The system fears only the one who records truth clearly and calmly because record removes room for lies.

This chapter explores the law of record, the rules that govern memory turned into writing. Understanding this principle allows you to see how councils and courts use documentation to create authority, and how you can use same process to protect peace and honour.

The first rule of record is that silence creates presumption. If you do not speak or write, the world assumes you agree. This principle existed long before modern government. In ancient commerce, if one merchant sent offer and other remained silent, silence was taken as acceptance. This rule still governs most transactions today. When you receive letter and do not reply, your silence confirms consent. The council knows this. Each demand it sends becomes contract if unanswered. The one who does not reply agrees without knowing it.

The second rule of record is that writing overrides speech. Words spoken can be forgotten or denied, but record remains. This is why officials insist that everything be put in writing. When you speak on phone, it means nothing in law. When you write and sign, it becomes evidence. The Sovereign must understand this and follow same discipline. Keep all communication written and preserved. Once you begin acting in writing, authority shifts from assumption to evidence.

The third rule of record is that truth must be timely. A record created too late loses strength. Law respects those who speak when needed, not those who wait until conflict grows. When letter arrives, reply in reasonable time. Date your reply. Keep proof of posting. Each step builds chain of evidence that cannot be broken by confusion or delay.

The fourth rule of record is that integrity gives power to document. Paper itself holds no authority. Ink and seal mean nothing without truth. A false statement, even when signed, carries no lawful force. A true statement, even when ignored, remains evidence forever. Honour gives life to record just as breath gives life to word.

To understand the system's dependence on record, watch how it behaves. Councils issue notices with dates, reference numbers, and signatures. Courts produce orders recorded by clerks. Banks rely on signed agreements to claim debt. None of them act without paper because paper becomes their memory. The moment you master same art, balance returns.

The Sovereign keeps private record not to imitate bureaucracy but to protect conscience. The difference lies in purpose. The council records to control. The living being records to preserve truth. One enslaves, the other frees. Yet both use same tools. The question is whose hand holds the pen.

The law of record also teaches patience. A document gains strength over time when unrebutted. When you send notice and receive no reply, your words mature into evidence. Time confirms truth. This principle is known as acquiescence. It means that silence maintained for reasonable period equals agreement. Councils rely on this. They send letters, wait for silence, and act upon it. You can do the same in peace. When you give notice of truth and receive no rebuttal, your record stands above assumption.

Memory fades with emotion. Record preserves clarity. When fear or anger cloud judgement, written truth restores order. This is why every Sovereign must discipline themselves to write, even when feeling uncertain. Writing calms the mind because it replaces confusion with structure. Each sentence brings you closer to understanding. The act of writing becomes act of law within yourself.

The system fears not violence but record. Violence can be dismissed as rebellion. Record cannot be dismissed because it reflects law's own process. The clerk who reads calm and dated letter feels its authority even if they pretend not to. They see reflection of their own procedure mirrored back at them. They know that one who writes calmly cannot be easily deceived.

Law also teaches that memory and record must align. If you say one thing and write another, confusion arises. Consistency is sign of integrity. Before you write, think clearly. Once written, stand by your word. Changing record weakens authority. Truth requires steadiness. Speak little, write less, mean every word.

The private record is not accumulation of paper but collection of moments of awareness. Each document captures instant when truth was seen clearly. These moments form pattern, and that pattern becomes story of honour. Councils have archives of control. You build archive of conscience. One uses fear to maintain obedience. The other uses peace to maintain truth.

Every notice or affidavit you create adds to your living record. The more you write, the stronger your memory becomes. You no longer depend on recollection to defend truth. You have proof. This removes anxiety because you can show exactly what happened. Law protects those who can demonstrate process. Record is that demonstration.

To illustrate power of record, consider simple exchange. A council claims payment. You reply with calm letter asking for contract and proof of obligation. They remain silent. Weeks pass. You keep their letter, your reply, and proof of delivery. If dispute arises later, your file speaks for you. You have truth recorded. They have assumption. Law stands with record, not with silence.

Memory fades, but paper remains. This is why the wise treat every letter as seed. Each one holds potential to grow into tree of evidence. Care for it with patience. File it with order. Label it clearly. The garden of your archive will one day protect you.

The law of record mirrors law of life. What you remember shapes what you believe. What you write shapes what others believe. When you write truthfully, you strengthen both. This is why record keeping is moral act as well as practical one. It trains honesty. The one who writes truth becomes truthful by habit.

The next chapter will explore how words themselves form evidence. It will show how precision of language turns record into lawful statement and how misunderstanding weakens even strongest truth. You will learn how to use language not to argue but to affirm. Once words are mastered, record becomes unbreakable.

Every council, court, and agency understands the law of record because it forms the backbone of their own authority. They never rely on memory. Every conversation, agreement, or payment is followed by confirmation in writing. The written document converts talk into proof. You see this everywhere. When you open bank account, you sign form. When you register for service, you confirm by signature. The act of writing transforms intention into contract. That principle works both ways.

If you write calmly, clearly, and truthfully, you create record as strong as theirs. The system relies on imbalance, believing that only its papers matter. When you create your own, that imbalance disappears. Two records now exist, one of authority and one of truth. Law must always consider both. It cannot ignore written testimony of living being.

The law of record has moral foundation. It rests on concept of remembrance. When you write, you honour truth by preserving it. Forgetfulness allows deceit to spread. Written record guards against forgetfulness. This is why many traditions treat writing as sacred. The word made visible carries same power as oath. The hand that writes truth joins conscience with form.

Many misunderstand purpose of record. They think of it as weapon to win dispute. That is mistake. Record is not for fighting but for protecting peace. It is statement of truth placed on paper so that conflict may end. Every letter you write should aim to clarify, not to accuse. The more clearly you write, the less room there is for misunderstanding. That is true remedy.

The law of record also connects to law of notice. To serve notice is to extend memory beyond yourself. When you send letter, you create event that cannot be undone. Whether or not the other party replies, notice exists. The system acknowledges receipt automatically because its own process depends on record of delivery. Thus, by using its tools, you bind it to your truth.

The strength of record depends on honesty of intention. Never write to manipulate or deceive. A record built on falsehood destroys itself. In long run, only truth survives scrutiny. If you make claim that cannot be supported, withdraw it quickly and correct record. Law respects correction made in good faith. It punishes deception but forgives sincerity.

Keep in mind that record begins long before you send letter. It starts in thought. Each idea becomes seed of future document. Before writing, ask yourself whether your intention is peace. If it is, proceed. If it is anger, wait. The energy with which you write remains within record. Calm words hold strength. Harsh words weaken truth by clouding it with emotion.

When you write, structure matters. Begin with statement of identity as living man or woman. Follow with clear description of event or issue. Present facts in order. Avoid speculation. End with declaration of peace. Example: "This communication is made in honour and without intent to cause harm." These words close door to conflict and keep tone of correspondence lawful.

Another aspect of the law of record is witness. When others see and confirm your actions, evidence gains depth. Two or three witnesses transform private act into public truth. This is why oaths and signatures carry weight. They extend your memory into memory of others. Witness converts individual truth into shared certainty.

In practice, not every document needs witness. Many notices and letters stand on their own. Yet for important statements, such as affidavits, witnessing adds force. When a friend or colleague signs as witness, they are not agreeing with content but confirming that you wrote and signed freely. That confirmation protects you from false accusation of fraud or coercion.

Records also gain power through order. An untidy archive weakens authority. Keep documents chronological. Use folders labelled by subject and year. Number pages when creating long statement. Include index page listing all correspondence. If ever you must present evidence, organisation speaks louder than emotion. The one with clear record earns respect.

Your personal archive is living memory of conscience. Each page reflects decision made in awareness. Over time, you will see pattern emerge. The same principles of honour, patience, and peace will repeat. That pattern becomes your personal law. It governs your actions without need for external authority. Law written within becomes law written without.

Never underestimate quiet strength of record. Officials often underestimate those who write calmly. They expect either silence or anger. When calm letter arrives citing truth without aggression, it unsettles them. It reminds them that power belongs to written word, not title. Some may ignore you, others may respond defensively, but all will know that you understand foundation of law.

Remember also that record protects both sides. It defends your honour but also prevents injustice against others. When all parties act in writing, truth becomes easier to see. Misunderstanding fades. Many conflicts vanish once both sides commit to record. This is how law brings peace when used properly.

The law of record operates beyond paper. It also governs your speech and action. Each time you speak truthfully, you create invisible record in conscience. Each time you lie, you damage it. The external archive reflects internal one. When both align, you live in peace. When they differ, confusion and fear appear. This is why lawful living begins within.

In the wider world, governments create archives of everything citizens do. They claim to preserve truth but often hide it. The Sovereign creates private archive openly to protect honesty. The difference lies in intent. Governments store information to maintain control. You store information to maintain integrity. Both act from memory, but only one acts from conscience.

Some may argue that keeping record invites attention from authority. The opposite is true. Those who act chaotically attract enforcement. Those who act with order appear responsible and reasonable. When your correspondence is calm, respectful, and well documented, it disarms hostility. Even within rigid systems, people respect professionalism. Peaceful conduct wins allies silently.

The more you practise record keeping, the more natural it becomes. You start to record conversations, dates, and details automatically. You no longer depend on memory that fades. You have proof of every stage of your journey. This confidence allows you to respond rather than react. The system cannot surprise you because you know your own history.

The law of record and memory is timeless. It served merchants in ancient markets, families in disputes, and travellers on their journeys. Today it serves you. By mastering it, you reclaim control of narrative that others seek to write for you. You become author rather than character in story of your life.

Record also connects generations. Your words today may guide others tomorrow. A child who finds letters written in honour learns what peace looks like on paper. The example lives beyond your lifetime. The written record becomes moral inheritance.

To live lawfully is to live remembered. The unrecorded life drifts into silence. The recorded life stands as example. Councils, courts, and corporations understand this and write their truth daily. The Sovereign does same but for higher reason. You write not to bind others but to free yourself.

The next chapter will explore how words themselves form substance of evidence. It will explain how truth expressed precisely cannot be twisted by interpretation. It will show that every letter is living witness, and every sentence a step toward peace.

Chapter 2:
Words as Evidence of Truth

Every record begins with word. Words shape law, define meaning, and carry truth from mind to page. They are not mere symbols; they are instruments of creation. The system understands this better than most. Councils, courts, and governments write laws with care because they know that what is written controls what is believed. The Sovereign must learn same discipline, to write not from fear or reaction but from awareness and precision.

When you write, you make statement that may outlive you. Your words can become evidence that protects or condemns. That is why honesty and clarity must guide every sentence. The man who writes without understanding creates confusion. The man who writes with truth creates record that cannot be shaken.

The first rule of words as evidence is accuracy. Law depends on definition. Every term used carries specific meaning. Confusion of language creates confusion of law. Councils rely on this. They use words like "person," "occupier," or "liable" knowing that few understand difference between common meaning and legal meaning. To protect yourself, learn to read carefully. Before you agree to anything, know what each word means within their system.

For example, the word "person" does not mean living man or woman. It refers to legal entity recognised by statute. When you accept label of person, you step into role created by legislation. That role carries duties and liabilities unknown to living being. One word changes entire relationship. Understanding this is foundation of lawful awareness.

The second rule is simplicity. Truth does not need complex language. Councils hide behind long sentences and formal tone to appear superior. The Sovereign writes plainly. Simple language carries more power because it cannot be twisted. When you say, "I require proof of contract," every reader understands meaning. When you write with unnecessary words, you invite interpretation. Clarity defeats deception.

The third rule is consistency. Your words must always reflect same truth. If one letter says you are willing to settle lawful obligation and another appears to deny obligation entirely, confusion arises. Confusion weakens standing. Always review what you have written before sending next letter. The private record must read as single voice of peace, not series of contradictions.

The fourth rule is tone. Law respects calmness. Aggressive words destroy authority. When you write in anger, your record reflects emotion rather than truth. Officials reading it see frustration and dismiss content. When you write calmly, even those who disagree sense strength. Tone reveals intent. Peaceful words carry moral force that commands respect silently.

The fifth rule is completeness. A half-truth is as dangerous as falsehood. When you state fact, ensure it is supported by evidence. Avoid exaggeration or speculation. If you cannot prove statement, phrase it as belief, not fact. Example: "It is my understanding that no contract exists." This keeps record honest while preserving peace. Law rewards accuracy and humility.

Words also hold spiritual weight. Every statement you make shapes your reality. When you declare truth in writing, you align conscience with law. This harmony gives power to paper beyond its material form. The man who writes truth becomes channel of law rather than subject of it. The more you practise truthful writing, the more naturally it flows.

To use words as evidence, learn difference between statement, declaration, and affidavit. A statement expresses view. A declaration affirms truth without oath. An affidavit swears truth under penalty of perjury. Each holds different level of force. Know when to use each. Use statement for correspondence, declaration for belief, and affidavit for evidence.

When you write declaration, avoid unnecessary adjectives or emotional phrases. Emotion weakens clarity. Truth does not need decoration. Example: "I declare that I have not entered any contract with council" is stronger than "I firmly declare with great certainty that I have never at any time ever entered any contract." Simplicity is proof of confidence.

Precision in words also protects you from misinterpretation. If you write, "I refuse to pay," the council may treat it as rebellion. If you write, "I am willing to settle any lawful obligation upon proof of claim," you remain in honour. The meaning changes entirely. The second phrase removes hostility and places burden on claimant. Words decide whether record speaks peace or conflict.

The power of definition cannot be overstated. In law, every argument begins and ends with meaning of words. Those who control language control outcome. This is why councils and governments constantly redefine terms. They change meaning of "payment," "ownership," and "consent" to suit policy. The Sovereign must reclaim authority by defining terms in their own record. You may include short glossary at start of important document. Example: "In this correspondence, 'living being' refers to man or woman of conscience and truth." Such definitions establish your jurisdiction of language.

Always read letters from councils carefully. Each sentence is crafted to create impression of obligation. Look for conditional words like "may," "must," and "will." These imply different degrees of force. "Must" indicates command under statute. "May" implies choice disguised as duty. Once you see difference, fear fades. You recognise that much of what appears compulsory is merely suggestion.

When responding, mirror their structure but replace assumption with clarity. Example: "You may believe I am liable for payment. I require proof of such liability before I can act." This returns conversation to level ground. You acknowledge their claim without submission. Each word acts as lever of balance.

The law of words also applies within yourself. The way you describe experience shapes how you feel. If you say, "They are attacking me," you create emotion of defence. If you say, "They have made offer I do not accept without proof," you create peace. Words determine energy of response. Conscious choice of language transforms fear into confidence.

The system has always used language to command thought. Statutes are spells written in plain sight. Each act of parliament begins with phrase "Be it enacted." The word "enact" means to make real through declaration. Law is therefore creation of reality through word. When you write truth, you enact your own law. You become legislator of conscience.

Understanding this does not mean rejecting all law. It means remembering that law serves life. Written truth aligns with natural order when it arises from peace. The system's mistake is that it writes to control. The Sovereign writes to clarify. Both use same tool, yet purpose defines outcome.

The private record is collection of written truths. Each letter, affidavit, and declaration becomes testimony of living being. Together they form body of evidence known as record of standing. The quality of your words determines strength of that body. Lazy or careless language weakens it. Careful and truthful language strengthens it.

To test your writing, imagine reading it aloud to stranger. Would they understand your point without further explanation? If yes, it is ready. If not, simplify. A lawful document must speak clearly to any reasonable reader. Complexity hides weakness. Simplicity reveals confidence.

The next section will explore how misused words create false law. It will explain how assumption of meaning allows deception to spread and how awareness of language returns power to its rightful place. Words are the building blocks of law, and once you learn to shape them consciously, you hold key to lawful living.

Words create worlds. The history of every civilisation begins with language. Law, religion, and culture all depend upon the written and spoken word. The system of governance today is built upon documents written long before any of us were born. Statutes, charters, and acts are simply collections of words arranged in deliberate order. Whoever controls those words controls perception of authority. The Sovereign learns to reclaim that control through understanding.

When councils issue letters, their intention is not communication but command. The language is chosen to generate fear, not clarity. Phrases like "failure to respond will result in action" are designed to produce reaction rather than thought. Yet if you study such sentences carefully, you notice that they carry no lawful force until you accept them. The threat exists only in belief. The law of words teaches that meaning arises through consent. If you do not consent, the words remain suggestion, not order.

Every man and woman has the right to define their own terms. When you write, you act as lawmaker within your private record. This act does not interfere with public law but establishes your own jurisdiction of conscience. For example, if you write that "I define 'lawful' as that which causes no harm or deceit," you are expressing moral standard. Anyone who communicates with you is bound to that definition when they reply without objection. This is silent contract through language. The council uses same method. You can too.

Understanding etymology strengthens this awareness. Words change meaning over time, often to serve those in power. The word "authority" once meant source of creation. Now it means power over others. The word "service" once meant act of help. Now it often means mechanism of control. When you study original meanings, you begin to see how language has been reshaped to limit thought. Restoring true meaning restores balance.

The law of words also warns against careless speech. Every promise made casually becomes energetic bond. Saying "I will" creates obligation. Saying "I might" leaves room for choice. The one who speaks without care binds themselves unintentionally. Councils exploit this through forms that ask you to confirm details. A simple "yes" written without understanding may create contract. Awareness before action prevents entanglement.

The power of word extends beyond paper. Each conversation builds unseen record within conscience. Speaking in truth reinforces peace. Speaking falsely divides mind against itself. When you say what you do not believe, you weaken authority of future words. The world responds to vibration of sincerity more than grammar of law. The clerk reading your letter feels calmness or anger behind it. They respond accordingly. This is why tone carries greater influence than logic.

The Sovereign's task is not to master every legal definition but to master clarity. Say only what you mean and mean only what you say. Law respects precision. The moment your writing becomes ambiguous, others interpret it for their own benefit. Councils write vaguely on purpose. Their letters mix command and suggestion so that fear fills the gap. When you reply with simple direct words, fear loses space to grow.

Every written word acts like seed. Once sent, it grows silently. If planted in anger, it bears confusion. If planted in peace, it bears order. Take time before posting letter. Read it aloud. Feel whether tone reflects peace. If not, rewrite until it does. Patience in writing saves many conflicts later.

Another lesson of the law of words is reflection. The language you use reveals your inner state. If you write with hostility, it shows lack of confidence. If you write with calm certainty, it shows understanding. Each document is mirror of mind at moment of writing. Keep copies not only for legal proof but also for self-study. Reading past letters teaches how much you have grown in awareness.

Words gain authority through repetition. Councils rely on this principle by sending multiple reminders. Each repetition reinforces belief in obligation. You can use same principle positively. When you write consistent truth across several letters, you create rhythm of honour. Repetition of truth becomes anchor that holds during confusion. Over time, even officials recognise integrity behind your words.

Many spiritual traditions teach that word is bond between heaven and earth. When you speak or write truthfully, you align with natural law. This alignment creates protection that no office can override. Those who lie, even with title or power, eventually face their own words returned as judgment. The universe itself operates through principle of correspondence. What is written in deceit must one day be corrected by truth.

You may notice that officials often avoid answering direct questions. This is not oversight but strategy. By avoiding clear language, they maintain control. When you write concise questions that require yes or no, you corner deception. Bureaucracy survives on ambiguity. Clarity is its undoing. Each precise question you write removes layer of illusion.

For example, if council demands payment, you may write: "Please confirm whether a lawful contract exists between your corporation and myself, bearing both signatures." This question leaves no space for evasion without revealing absence of evidence. If they reply with reference to policy, they have not answered. Silence or misdirection becomes proof of dishonour. The power lies not in threat but in precision of question.

Your own understanding of grammar also matters. Many misunderstand meaning of simple punctuation. A full stop ends thought. A comma extends it. Misplaced punctuation can change entire sense of sentence. Councils exploit this through long paragraphs that mix conditions and exceptions. Break their structure down. Read one clause at time. Clarity will reveal weakness in argument.

When writing, favour short sentences. Each should carry one idea. This mirrors way law is written when it seeks truth rather than control. Ancient codes of honour used simple statements such as "Do no harm." Modern legislation hides behind pages of complexity. Return to simplicity, and your record will carry moral strength beyond measure.

The more you study power of language, the more you see it everywhere. Advertising, media, and politics all manipulate meaning to shape thought. Freedom begins with reclaiming language. When you define words by conscience rather than policy, you reclaim mind from confusion. The Sovereign who masters words cannot be deceived.

The final aspect of words as evidence is silence. Silence itself is word unspoken. When you choose not to reply, you speak through absence. In law, silence can mean acceptance or refusal depending on context. The wise use silence deliberately. After sending clear notice, remain silent until reply arrives. Silence in peace confirms strength. Silence in fear invites presumption. The difference lies in intent.

To use words lawfully, you must also use silence wisely. Together they form language of truth. Speak when clarification is needed. Write when record must exist. Remain silent when truth needs no defence. This balance is art of lawful living.

When truth governs word, and word governs record, law becomes expression of life rather than weapon of control. Councils, courts, and corporations will continue to write their rules, but the living being who understands language walks freely among them. They may send letters, but those letters no longer command fear. Each becomes opportunity to practise honour through word.

The next chapter will explore how private communication and public silence interact. It will explain how to protect truth within correspondence and why the most powerful record often exists unseen by system that ignores it. The law of words prepares ground for that deeper understanding. Once you master language, you are ready to master silence.

Chapter 3: Private Communication and Public Silence

Lawful communication is not performance for public approval. It is private act between living beings who recognise truth. The power of record comes from integrity of correspondence, not from audience. Councils, courts, and corporations act through public channels that appear transparent but are built on procedure, not honesty. The Sovereign acts through private correspondence rooted in conscience. This is where truth lives and where peace begins.

When you write to council or agency, you enter private communication. Though addressed to public body, your letter is personal notice between man or woman and institution. This distinction matters. Public speech demands permission. Private correspondence operates under natural law. It requires only good faith and clarity. Once you understand this, fear of authority fades. You realise that every official is simply correspondent bound by same duty of honour.

The principle of privacy protects conscience. Public systems function through policy. They treat individuals as data within category. Private communication restores individuality. It reminds both parties that behind title and signature stands living being. When you write personally, using calm and measured words, you awaken humanity within structure. Officials may ignore, but they can never truly forget tone of honour.

Private record also shields truth from distortion. Public forums twist meaning through opinion and interpretation. Private correspondence preserves words exactly as written. It is your truth unedited. When you send letter by recorded delivery, you create closed circle of communication between you and recipient. This circle cannot be broken by speculation. It stands as contract of honour sealed by intention.

Many misunderstand idea of public silence. They expect councils or courts to announce truth openly. Yet public silence is their defence. When confronted by lawful question, they retreat into quietness, pretending that absence of response means nothing. In fact, silence speaks louder than denial. Law recognises silence as form of agreement when honourable question remains unanswered. This is why patience is strength of Sovereign.

To use silence effectively, you must first create opportunity for it. This requires clear question or notice. Once written and served, time becomes witness. Each day without reply strengthens record. When period stated in notice passes, silence matures into evidence. The council's failure to respond becomes proof of absence of contract. This is not magic; it is logic. Law operates on presumption until evidence replaces it. Your notice replaces presumption with fact of unanswered question.

Public silence differs from private peace. Public silence hides fear. Private peace rests on understanding. When you act from awareness, you do not need public confirmation. You know truth because you have record of process. This inner calm separates living being from crowd. The crowd seeks validation. The Sovereign seeks clarity.

Never seek recognition from those who profit from confusion. The value of your record does not depend on approval from system. Truth requires no audience. When you write notice in peace, you fulfil duty to conscience. Whether council replies or not, your integrity remains intact. That is the real victory.

The system operates through illusion of public dialogue. Councils publish statements and reports that appear transparent. Yet all such documents are written to maintain appearance of fairness, not to reveal truth. The private record of living being stands outside that theatre. It carries quiet authority that no headline can erase.

You will notice that officials avoid private correspondence once conversation becomes too precise. They prefer generic letters signed by "Customer Services" or "Legal Department." This depersonalisation protects them from responsibility. To restore accountability, address your letters personally whenever possible. Use name of officer and position held. When they receive personal letter, they face moral choice. Ignoring it becomes act of dishonour rather than routine procedure.

Private communication requires patience and dignity. Never write with intent to expose or embarrass. Write to clarify, not to win. Each letter should carry tone of goodwill. Phrases such as "I write in peace and honour seeking resolution" disarm hostility before it begins. Law respects those who act with fairness. Even within rigid institutions, honour commands quiet respect.

You must also learn art of restraint. Not every letter deserves reply. Once you have stated truth clearly and received silence, repetition weakens position. Record speaks through time, not volume. The system floods you with letters to exhaust attention. Respond only when new claim arises. Each unnecessary reply risks reopening matter you already closed. The wise keep silence once record is complete.

The balance between communication and silence mirrors rhythm of breath. You inhale by writing. You exhale by waiting. Both are essential. Too much writing suffocates clarity. Too much silence invites presumption. Harmony lies in alternating them with awareness.

When you write, protect your privacy physically as well as lawfully. Keep all correspondence within secure space. Label and file letters chronologically. Treat archive as sacred trust, not collection of paper. Each document represents exchange of truth between souls, even when one side denies it. Handle them with care and respect. This attitude strengthens spiritual power of record.

Privacy also means discernment in sharing. Do not broadcast your letters or affidavits publicly unless necessary. The moment record enters public domain, it becomes subject to interpretation and ridicule. Keep it private until silence itself becomes story worth telling. When truth needs witness, reveal it calmly, without anger. Let record speak; you remain quiet.

Public silence can tempt frustration. You may wonder whether efforts matter when replies never come. They do. Every unanswered letter is proof of system's dependence on fear rather than law. Each silence exposes lack of contract. You are not seeking approval; you are documenting truth. The council's silence is your evidence, not your failure.

The law of honour rewards patience. In time, pattern of silence forms undeniable record. When many letters remain unanswered, even within bureaucracy, weight of silence becomes heavy. Officials may shift tone or withdraw claim quietly. They will not admit defeat, but they will retreat. Your peace becomes mirror that reveals their noise.

Communication through private record transforms energy of conflict. Instead of shouting in public square, you write in calm room. Instead of seeking to prove others wrong, you affirm your own truth. This shift removes fear because you no longer depend on outcome. You know that each letter adds strength to archive of honour.

There is beauty in lawful silence. It is not absence of speech but presence of certainty. It says, "I have spoken truth. I wait in peace." Those who live by procedure cannot understand this strength. They interpret silence as weakness because they fear stillness. Yet in stillness, truth gathers force.

The Sovereign who understands both communication and silence lives beyond reach of control. Councils thrive on reaction. Courts feed on argument. When you stop reacting and start recording, their nourishment disappears. They cannot feed on peace.

To practise this balance, create rhythm in correspondence. When letter arrives, wait one day before reading again. Respond only after understanding its intent. Then write short, factual notice. Close with statement of peace. File everything and forget it. Silence will work in your favour.

Private communication and public silence are twin pillars of lawful living. They reflect same principle found in nature. Rivers speak through movement, yet oceans hold silence of depth. The wise man becomes both. His words flow with purpose, his silence holds truth.

The next section will explore how these principles form foundation of lawful record. You will learn how to create correspondence that commands respect, how to use silence as evidence, and how to remain at peace when public systems refuse to acknowledge truth.

Private communication exists so that truth may travel quietly. It does not seek audience or applause. It serves purpose of correction. Each letter written in peace is small act of repair in world ruled by confusion. The Sovereign does not argue with system; they converse with conscience. The record of that conversation becomes living proof of awareness.

Every official letter you receive carries hidden invitation. It says, without words, "Will you respond as person or as living being?" If you reply with anger, you respond as person bound by emotion. If you reply with clarity and calmness, you respond as living being governed by truth. The choice belongs to you each time you open envelope.

When you write privately, you speak from position of equality. You do not stand beneath authority or above it. You stand beside it, as one living being addressing another. This balance changes energy of exchange. Fear dissolves because both sides become human. Officials are not prepared for this. They expect resistance or silence, not calmness. The one who writes peacefully confuses structure built on control.

Public silence reveals much about nature of power. The system survives through performance of confidence. It must appear certain even when uncertain. When confronted by question that exposes weakness, it falls silent. This silence is not victory for them but surrender. Yet most people misinterpret it. They panic, thinking no response means failure. In truth, silence is confession. Law sees it as admission that no lawful answer exists.

To use public silence lawfully, always set clear terms in your communication. For example, you may write, "If no reply is received within twenty-one days, it shall be taken as confirmation that no contract exists between us." This creates lawful condition. When time passes, their silence fulfils condition automatically. The record now carries presumption of agreement. You need do nothing further.

Some fear that silence from authority might later turn into action. This fear arises from misunderstanding. If your record shows you acted in honour and gave fair opportunity for reply, any later action becomes evidence of bad faith on their part. Law protects good faith when documented. Your peace becomes shield against injustice.

Never use public silence to boast. Truth does not need declaration of victory. Quietly continue with life. The purpose of lawful communication is restoration of peace, not display of defiance. When council or agency stops writing, that is end of conversation. Do not seek to reopen it through pride. Let silence be closure.

Silence can also be inner discipline. It teaches patience and detachment. The one who can remain silent without anxiety has mastered self. The council may send repeated demands or warnings. Each one tests your peace. Respond only when new claim arises. Each unnecessary reply gives them power. Discipline in silence trains mind to recognise difference between demand and offer.

Private communication requires awareness of timing. Respond too quickly and you may miss hidden meaning. Wait too long and silence may be misread as consent. Balance lies in awareness of intent behind letter. Read every document twice, once for words, once for tone. The first reveals claim, the second reveals emotion. Respond only to claim, never to emotion.

You will encounter people who misunderstand your silence. They may think you are avoiding responsibility. Explain calmly that you are waiting for lawful proof before acting. Truth needs no defence, only evidence. Those who act from fear fill silence with noise. Those who act from understanding let silence reveal truth naturally.

Privacy also protects dignity. When you keep communication between you and correspondent, you avoid gossip and distraction. Sharing private letters with others invites judgement. Outsiders project their own fear and confusion onto your process. The fewer people involved, the clearer your path remains. Record grows strongest in quiet soil.

If you must involve witness, choose one who understands peace. A witness filled with anger weakens energy of process. They may twist meaning of words or speak unnecessarily. Select witness who values truth above opinion. The presence of such person strengthens integrity of record.

Public silence often frightens those who expect immediate justice. The system teaches impatience. It measures success by reaction. True law works differently. It grows slowly like tree. Its roots form unseen before fruit appears. When you act in peace, your result may come quietly months later. Trust timing of truth.

When truth is written, it does not vanish. It lingers in collective memory of system. Clerks move between departments, officers change roles, but your letter remains in archive. Each time new hand touches file, they see calmness and clarity. Some feel spark of conscience. Change begins unseen. This is how private record transforms public silence into slow awakening.

Communication in peace heals more than disputes. It restores balance within yourself. Writing trains patience, accuracy, and empathy. Silence trains faith, humility, and strength. Together they refine character of Sovereign. Without this inner refinement, knowledge of law becomes mere weapon. With it, knowledge becomes wisdom.

There is danger in overexposure. Many who study lawful principles fall into habit of broadcasting every thought online. They seek validation through followers and comments. Yet public debate drains energy and invites misunderstanding. Lawful communication loses purity when shared for entertainment. Keep process sacred. Share insight only with those who ask sincerely.

Public silence, when observed collectively, can become act of unity. Imagine community of living men and women refusing to feed argument with anger. Their shared silence would reveal emptiness of authority louder than any protest. Power expects confrontation; it cannot comprehend quiet understanding.

Silence also gives space for inspiration. When mind stops demanding reaction, truth rises naturally. Many discover best words during stillness that follows first impulse to reply. The art of lawful communication is therefore art of waiting. You write from clarity that comes after emotion, not before it.

To maintain balance, set rhythm of correspondence for yourself. Decide how long you will wait before replying to any letter. Mark dates clearly. This discipline prevents system from controlling your time. Their urgency becomes irrelevant. You respond according to your own measure of peace. This is sovereignty in practice.

When correspondence ends, close file properly. Write short note summarising event and date of final silence. Place it on top of folder. This marks completion in both record and mind. Unfinished matters drain energy. Finished ones restore it. Closure through silence is law's quiet gift.

Public silence will continue to exist as long as systems fear accountability. Yet each unanswered letter weakens wall of secrecy. Bit by bit, honourable communication erodes ignorance. No authority can resist truth forever. Silence delays but cannot destroy it.

You may never receive written apology from those who ignored you, yet peace itself becomes proof of success. The absence of conflict is sign that honour has done its work. You stand free not because world acknowledged it but because conscience did.

The next chapter will show how notices, affidavits, and declarations transform private truth into structured evidence. You will see how these instruments link communication and silence into chain of honour. Through them, record becomes living testimony of lawful being.

Chapter 4:
Notices, Affidavits, and Declarations

The written word gains authority through structure. Private record becomes lawful evidence when shaped into form that expresses truth clearly. Three forms stand above all others: the notice, the affidavit, and the declaration. Each serves unique purpose, yet all share same foundation of honour. Together they form triangle of lawful communication. When understood and used with sincerity, they become instruments of peace rather than weapons of conflict.

A **notice** is written communication that informs another of fact, intention, or condition. It carries no hostility. It merely states truth or request for clarification. Its power lies in service and silence. When notice is served properly and receives no reply, it becomes evidence of acquiescence. Law accepts unrebutted notice as truth. Councils and agencies rely on same principle when sending demands. You can use it peacefully for protection rather than control.

The **affidavit** is written statement of truth sworn or affirmed before witness. It carries highest weight in law because it binds conscience of author. It is oath to truth itself. The strength of affidavit comes not from paper or signature but from honour of writer. Once signed, it stands as living testimony. If unrebutted, it becomes conclusive evidence. Even court cannot overturn it without counter affidavit of equal standing.

A **declaration** is written affirmation of belief, right, or intent. It does not require oath or witness, yet it carries lawful force through sincerity. It is formal announcement to world of where you stand. Declarations express authority of conscience without confrontation. Examples include declaration of independence, declaration of peace, or declaration of status. Each confirms awareness of self.

Understanding difference between these three forms allows you to communicate truth in precise manner. Confusion between them weakens record. The notice invites response. The affidavit confirms truth. The declaration proclaims intent. When used together, they build chain of honour that transforms private understanding into documented law.

To create effective notice, begin with simple structure. Write title at top such as "Notice of Inquiry" or "Notice of Conditional Acceptance." State clearly what you are addressing and what you require. Avoid emotion. List facts in order. Include reasonable time for reply, usually between fourteen and twenty-one days. End with statement such as, "Failure to respond will be taken as confirmation of agreement." Sign and date. Keep copy and proof of delivery. Once served, wait patiently.

The secret of notice lies in patience. Its power grows with time, not repetition. Each day without reply strengthens record. When period expires, you may write second letter titled "Notice of Default." This confirms that first notice stands unrebutted. Together they form lawful pair: offer and confirmation. The system itself uses same pattern in its correspondence. You are simply returning process to rightful balance.

When writing affidavit, remember that it represents oath to truth. Never include anything you cannot personally confirm. Speculation has no place in affidavit. Begin with words, "I, a living man or woman, affirm the following to be true to best of my knowledge and belief." Then number each statement. Each line should contain single fact or observation. End with statement of truth and your signature. If possible, sign before witness who adds their own signature. This witness need not be official; any honest person will do.

Affidavit stands as evidence even without external validation because it comes from conscience. In law, truth unrebutted stands as fact. When you serve affidavit upon another and receive no counter affidavit, your testimony becomes lawful record. This principle of equal standing preserves fairness. One truth can only be challenged by another truth, not by opinion or silence.

The declaration differs from both notice and affidavit. It is statement of identity and purpose. Through declaration, you remind yourself and others of who you are. It sets tone for all future correspondence. Declarations may affirm living status, intent to act in peace, or commitment to lawful conduct. They are not reactive but creative. You write them before conflict arises. They define boundary of conscience.

For example, you may write declaration that begins, "I, a living woman, declare my commitment to act always in peace and to require proof of claim before honouring any demand." This simple statement transforms fear into confidence. It reminds reader that your actions follow principle, not panic. Declarations serve as moral compass. They keep communication aligned with purpose.

Each of these instruments relies on same element: service. To serve document means to deliver it in manner that creates proof of receipt. Recorded post or personal delivery with witness are common methods. The act of service transforms private writing into lawful record. Without service, document remains private note. With service, it becomes communication recognised by law.

Service must be done respectfully. The aim is to inform, not to intimidate. Never use red ink or threatening symbols. These cause fear and reduce credibility. Simplicity and calm design command more respect than decoration. The paper itself should be clean and plain. Law responds to substance, not theatre.

Order also matters. Notices usually come first, followed by affidavits if necessary, and then declarations to reaffirm position. This sequence mirrors natural flow of communication: question, proof, and conclusion. By following this order, your record gains logical strength. Anyone reading it later will see process of fairness.

Remember that these documents are tools of peace. They exist to prevent conflict, not to create it. When used in anger, they lose power. The affidavit written with malice becomes hollow. The notice filled with accusation invites defence rather than dialogue. The declaration made to boast loses spiritual value. Always check your intention before writing. The most powerful document is one written in love of truth.

The next section will explore deeper meaning of these forms, showing how each reflects different aspect of human nature and law. You will see that notices speak from intellect, affidavits from conscience, and declarations from spirit. When all three unite, record becomes complete reflection of living being.

Each document you create carries a piece of your awareness. When written in truth, it represents different part of your being. The notice speaks through reason, the affidavit speaks through conscience, and the declaration speaks through intention. Together they form complete reflection of the living man or woman acting in honour. Understanding how these parts work in harmony is essential for building private record that holds lawful power.

The **notice** is intellectual. It appeals to reason and order. It presents question or demand for proof without emotion. Its tone is firm but calm. The purpose of notice is to remove confusion. When you send notice, you say, "Let us bring light where there is assumption." It is invitation to truth. Many who learn about sovereignty think notice is weapon. In truth, it is act of peace. The one who sends notice extends opportunity for correction. That is honour in action.

The **affidavit** belongs to conscience. It comes from inner witness that cannot lie. To write affidavit truthfully requires courage. You place your reputation upon the words. This commitment transforms paper into moral instrument. It says, "I am willing to stand by this truth even under scrutiny." The system fears affidavit because it binds conscience, not policy. Officials may ignore it, but in law it remains unrebutted testimony.

The **declaration** belongs to spirit. It announces what you are and what you choose to stand for. It does not require evidence or response. It is self-existing truth. Declaration frees you from need for external validation. Once declared, your position becomes foundation for all communication. It brings unity between thought, word, and action.

Understanding these levels helps you maintain balance. Some rely only on notices and grow frustrated when silence follows. They forget that notice alone lacks heart. Others rely on declarations but never act, leaving truth untested. A few write affidavits impulsively and regret words later. Harmony comes when all three work together. Notice seeks clarity, affidavit confirms truth, and declaration sets moral tone.

When you begin any matter, start with declaration of intent. This reminds you of your purpose. Then issue notice to invite response. If silence follows, record becomes proof. Finally, if needed, write affidavit to confirm truth under oath. This process mirrors natural law. Intention gives birth to action, action gives rise to evidence, and evidence matures into truth.

Each document should include clear identification. Always write your full name followed by phrase "a living man" or "a living woman." This distinguishes you from corporate title. Use physical address for correspondence but avoid implying residence within jurisdiction of corporation. Example: "Mail for service may be sent to care of (address)." This wording allows communication without submission.

Clarity of structure protects you from misinterpretation. Begin every document with heading stating type of paper and purpose. Example: "Notice of Conditional Acceptance regarding claim reference number." The reader immediately understands subject. Number paragraphs to aid reference. Close with signature, printed name, and date. If witnessed, include witness signature below yours with statement of observation. Keep language consistent across all documents in matter.

Affidavits deserve particular care. Once signed, they cannot be withdrawn without explanation. Before writing, reflect deeply on every statement. Ask whether it is factual, observed, or believed. Label accordingly. For example, "To my knowledge," "In my experience," or "I believe this to be true." These phrases show honesty of scope. Overstatement weakens affidavit because it invites easy rebuttal. Precision protects integrity.

When you serve affidavit, include covering letter or short notice of service stating what it is and why it is sent. Example: "Please find enclosed my affidavit of truth regarding correspondence dated (date). This affidavit stands as unrebutted evidence unless counter affidavit is received within fourteen days." This provides clear timeline and condition. Keep proof of delivery in your archive.

Declaration writing requires awareness of tone. Avoid grand or theatrical statements. The purpose is not to impress but to affirm. Simple words spoken from heart carry more strength than elaborate language. Example: "I declare that I live by truth and honour, causing no harm and seeking peace with all." Such declaration becomes anchor for conduct. It reminds you daily of standard you set for yourself.

These three forms also train discipline. They require patience, accuracy, and humility. Each teaches virtue necessary for lawful living. The notice teaches patience because it demands waiting. The affidavit teaches accuracy because it requires truth. The declaration teaches humility because it asks no reply. Through them, you learn to master self before mastering system.

Another aspect of lawful communication is record of sequence. Each document builds upon previous one. Keep clear timeline showing when each was written, served, and received. This chronology becomes shield when facing confusion or accusation. Law respects process shown in order. Random letters without structure appear chaotic. Ordered correspondence demonstrates responsibility.

Your private record will eventually contain many notices, affidavits, and declarations. Treat it as library of your conscience. Review it periodically. Reading older documents reminds you of progress in awareness. You may see where emotion once influenced tone and how peace has replaced it. This reflection strengthens faith in truth.

Never copy templates blindly. Many documents shared online claim to provide instant remedy. Most contain errors or exaggerated claims. True lawful communication must come from your understanding, not imitation. Read examples to learn structure, then write in your own words. Authenticity gives power that borrowed phrases lack. The record must sound like your voice, not echo of another.

If you receive affidavit or notice from another, respond with same level of respect you expect for your own. Read carefully and reply honestly. If claim is false, rebut it with clear facts. If true, acknowledge it. Honour works both ways. Lawful living means treating others as you wish to be treated. This mutual respect forms unseen foundation of peace.

When writing any of these documents, remember that law serves life. Words written without compassion become empty. The notice written to intimidate loses moral force. The affidavit filled with pride becomes fragile. The declaration made without conviction fades quickly. Purity of intent determines lasting value of record.

The act of writing notice, affidavit, or declaration also has inward effect. It disciplines mind, purifies emotion, and strengthens conscience. Each document becomes mirror reflecting how deeply you understand truth. The process itself transforms you from student into practitioner of honour.

Through consistent practice, you will find that fewer notices are needed. Silence itself will begin to speak for you because your reputation becomes known. The one who writes always in peace gains respect even among officials. They may not agree with your philosophy, but they will recognise integrity. That recognition brings quiet protection.

The next chapter will explore how to build and maintain archive of honour. It will show how to preserve your documents properly, how to organise them into coherent record, and how this discipline strengthens both lawful standing and inner peace. The private archive becomes living memory of truth and cornerstone of sovereignty.

Chapter 5: Building the Archive of Honour

The private record has no value unless preserved with care. Truth written but lost is truth wasted. To hold power, your documents must live in order, not in piles of confusion. The archive is foundation of lawful standing. It is memory of every act of honour, kept so that no lie can erase it. When built with discipline and peace, the archive becomes mirror of your integrity. It shows the world, and more importantly yourself, that your life is guided by conscience and clarity.

Every system on earth keeps records because record is source of authority. Governments hold registers, banks keep ledgers, and councils maintain files. They use these archives to justify actions. The Sovereign does the same but for opposite purpose. The state records to control. The Sovereign records to remember truth. Both act from same law of evidence, yet motive determines outcome. The state stores paper to preserve power. The Sovereign stores paper to preserve peace.

Begin by recognising that your archive is sacred space. It is not storage but sanctuary. Each letter, affidavit, and declaration is fragment of truth captured in time. Treat them with respect. Keep them clean, dry, and safe. Handle them with same care you would give to valuable book or family heirloom. The archive will one day tell story of your journey toward honour.

Start with physical organisation. Use folders or binders made of strong material. Divide them by subject. One for councils, one for banks, one for personal declarations, and one for general notices. Label each folder clearly on the spine and front. Write titles in calm handwriting or use printed labels. Avoid excessive decoration. Simplicity reflects peace.

Inside each folder, order documents chronologically. Place earliest letter at front and latest at back. This allows anyone reading to follow story easily. Number each page at bottom right corner. When adding new document, update index sheet at beginning of folder. The index should list document title, date written, date served, and method of service. This single page becomes map of your record.

Every document that leaves your hand should be copied. Keep original in folder and send duplicate. Use photocopy or scan. When receiving replies, file them immediately behind your own letter. Each exchange forms pair, representing question and answer. Over time, pattern of communication becomes clear. You will see when honour was shown and when it was ignored.

Proof of service is essential part of archive. Keep receipts from post office, delivery slips, and any tracking confirmation. Staple or clip them to corresponding letters. If possible, print digital confirmation pages showing delivery date. These small slips of paper often carry more legal weight than long arguments. They show that process was followed with precision.

For digital record, create mirrored structure on computer. Make folders with same titles as physical ones. Save documents as PDF files to prevent alteration. Name each file by date and subject, such as "2025-03-14 Notice to Council." Back up regularly on separate drive or secure cloud service. Technology may fail; truth must not.

Discipline in record keeping prevents confusion during stress. When letter of demand arrives, you can check archive calmly instead of reacting in fear. You will know whether issue has already been addressed. You will find copy of previous reply, proof of delivery, and any unanswered notice. This order transforms anxiety into confidence.

Regular maintenance strengthens habit. Once a week, spend short time reviewing archive. Remove duplicates or drafts no longer needed. Ensure documents remain in correct order. Read one or two old letters aloud. This practice keeps memory fresh and reminds you how far you have come in clarity.

Do not underestimate spiritual value of this discipline. Each act of filing, numbering, and labelling strengthens connection between thought and action. You train mind to move with order. The archive becomes reflection of inner world. A peaceful archive indicates peaceful heart. A chaotic one mirrors confusion. Treat order as meditation, not burden.

The archive also teaches humility. It reveals mistakes and lessons. Sometimes you will read old letter written in frustration and see lack of patience. Keep it. Do not destroy evidence of growth. The record of imperfection shows journey toward honour. Law respects transparency. The one who hides error betrays truth. The one who acknowledges it shows strength.

Another key principle is accessibility. Your archive must be understandable to others if ever required. Imagine someone else reading it after you. Would they see clear story? Would they understand your intention? If yes, your record is complete. If not, simplify structure. Add brief summary page explaining purpose of each folder. Clarity ensures that truth survives even when you are absent.

Store archive in safe place, protected from fire, moisture, and theft. Consider waterproof box or secure cabinet. Avoid leaving papers in damp or cluttered areas. Respect for record is respect for truth. Treat it as living companion, not pile of paper.

The private archive also extends to external memory. If trusted friend or relative understands your work, let them know where documents are kept. This prevents loss in case of emergency. Trust only those who value peace and confidentiality. A careless helper can undo years of careful order.

Be mindful that archive holds energy of its content. Letters written in anger or fear may carry heavy feeling. To balance this, include positive declarations and affirmations among them. Statements of peace and gratitude cleanse space spiritually. Over time, atmosphere around archive becomes calm. Entering that space reminds you of purpose behind every word.

Some prefer to include personal reflections in archive. This can be simple notebook describing thoughts and feelings during process. Writing reflection alongside official letters adds human context. It turns collection of documents into living story of transformation. Future readers will see not only what you wrote but how you grew.

The physical archive may one day be challenged or inspected. If that happens, remain calm. Present documents politely and confidently. Do not argue or explain unnecessarily. Let record speak. The one with organised archive commands respect even before opening folder. Officials recognise discipline of order. Many lose confidence when facing calm evidence.

Over time, your archive will grow large. Resist temptation to discard early work. Those first letters contain seeds of learning. Keep them as reminder of beginnings. The record is not just legal protection but teacher. Reading it reveals cycles of misunderstanding and correction. Each mistake resolved adds another layer of wisdom.

The act of building archive transforms how you see world. You begin noticing how every institution depends on same principle. Banks keep ledgers, schools keep registers, courts keep transcripts. Record is universal law of accountability. By keeping your own, you stand equal with any authority. You no longer fear accusation because your memory exists outside your mind.

When archive becomes habit, peace follows naturally. Life feels lighter because uncertainty fades. You know where everything stands. You trust your own process. This confidence radiates into every part of living. Others sense it. Conversations become calmer. Decisions become easier. Truth recorded brings stability that no external power can shake.

The next section will explore advanced care of archive, including indexing by subject, cross-referencing, and creating summary statements. It will also discuss how private archive connects to collective memory of community and why preservation of truth today ensures freedom for tomorrow.

The archive of honour does not end with tidy folders or labelled files. It is living system of memory that grows as your understanding grows. Each letter, declaration, and affidavit you file becomes thread in tapestry of truth. To maintain its strength, you must keep pattern consistent. Without discipline, record turns into clutter. With discipline, it becomes body of evidence that no authority can deny.

Indexing is key to mastery. Create single binder or document called "Master Index." This serves as directory for entire archive. Divide it into sections matching main folders: councils, banks, personal, and other. Under each, list document titles with short summaries. For example, "Notice of Conditional Acceptance to City Council regarding account reference," followed by date of service. The Master Index allows you to find any paper within minutes.

Cross-referencing adds depth. Sometimes one document connects to another in different folder. For instance, affidavit may support notice sent months earlier. In that case, write small note in margin or add reference number linking them. This interconnection turns archive into network of evidence rather than pile of paper. Law favours organisation because it mirrors logic.

When you close matter, create summary statement. Title it "Record of Resolution." List key events, documents sent, replies received, and final silence or agreement. Keep it on top of folder as overview. Anyone reading will understand full process without searching through every page. This saves time and shows responsibility.

Preserve your archive not only for defence but also for education. Future generations will learn from example. They will see that honour is not theory but practice. The letters you write today become textbooks for those who follow. Treat them accordingly.

Consider also moral effect of your archive on community. Every person who learns to record truth contributes to culture of accountability. When enough individuals keep accurate private records, deceit loses power. Councils and corporations rely on confusion. Clear documentation removes hiding places. Honour spreads quietly through example rather than protest.

There is beauty in seeing entire shelf of folders representing years of lawful living. Each one tells story of patience and perseverance. You can open any file and trace path of truth step by step. This visible memory gives peace that cannot be bought. It proves to you that order exists even in world of chaos.

Be cautious of digital dependency. Technology offers convenience but not permanence. Hard drives fail, accounts close, and access can be restricted. Maintain paper copies of most important documents. Ink on paper is proof that survives system failures. The simplest printed letter may one day protect you when digital systems fall silent.

When updating archive, use same care with additions as you did with first entries. New learning may tempt you to rewrite past documents. Resist urge to alter record. Truth evolves through correction, not erasure. If update is necessary, write new document titled "Addendum" or "Clarification." Attach it to original with clear note referencing both dates. This preserves integrity of timeline.

Avoid mixing personal and public correspondence within same folder. Keep clear separation between private life and lawful record. Personal notes, bills, or unrelated papers dilute authority of archive. The more focused each section remains, the stronger impression of professionalism it creates.

The archive also functions as compass. During difficult times, reading past letters reminds you of values that guide life. You see how often truth triumphed through patience rather than struggle. Each example renews faith in process of honour. The archive becomes quiet mentor, whispering lessons through pages.

Some people create second archive for community work. This may include minutes of meetings, notices served collectively, or declarations of assembly. Such collective archive requires shared discipline. Appoint one guardian responsible for accuracy and security. Trust is essential because once community archive loses integrity, entire effort collapses. Transparency and honesty must guide every entry.

For spiritual balance, dedicate small area in your home for archive. Keep it clean and free of clutter. You may place simple symbol of peace or candle nearby to remind you that this is not collection of conflict but shrine of understanding. Before adding new document, pause and reflect on intention. Ask yourself whether it serves truth or ego. Only record what serves peace.

You may wish to keep written logbook tracking when each document is filed or removed. This running journal adds human voice to archive. It captures mood and reflection of each moment. Years later, you will read those notes and recall emotions that once felt heavy but now seem light. It shows growth of soul alongside growth of record.

When you review archive, avoid attachment to outcome of past cases. Some matters may have ended without clear resolution. Accept that silence itself was answer. The purpose of record is not victory but preservation of truth. Let unfinished stories rest. They are reminders that law, like life, moves in its own time.

The archive of honour also protects reputation. Should anyone accuse you falsely, your organised record demonstrates character. It shows you act with consistency, patience, and respect. No argument can compete with visible proof of integrity. Officials may disagree with your philosophy but will respect discipline of process.

It is wise to include in archive copy of main principles guiding you. This may be short statement outlining your beliefs about law, honour, and peace. Place it at beginning of Master Index. It introduces reader to spirit behind entire collection. Anyone reviewing will understand context of your actions. This prevents misinterpretation of motive.

As years pass, you will notice that fewer new folders are required. This does not mean progress has slowed; it means mastery has grown. Once principles of honour become natural, need for defence decreases. The archive then transforms from shield into monument of understanding.

Building archive is lifelong commitment. It matures as you do. The young Sovereign begins with confusion, gathering papers uncertainly. With experience, order replaces fear. The mature Sovereign adds only what truly matters. Each stage teaches patience.

Preservation of truth extends beyond paper and ink. Speak truth in daily life. Keep record through honesty of word and action. The physical archive mirrors invisible one written in conscience. When both align, your life itself becomes lawful document. Every gesture, every word, every silence forms part of living record of peace.

When you live this way, you become embodiment of law. Councils may write statutes, but your life writes example. Archive becomes symbol of that example. It reminds you that order begins within.

The next chapter will explore concept of signature, oath, and witnessing under title "The Seal of the Living Word." It will show how living being gives life to record through act of signing, and how integrity behind signature defines its power.

Chapter 6:
The Seal of the Living Word

The signature is the bridge between thought and record. It is the mark that transforms words from expression into commitment. The living man or woman gives life to paper through this act of confirmation. Without signature, record is mere idea. With it, record becomes testimony of conscience. The seal of the living word is therefore not simple mark of name but statement of truth made visible.

Long before modern writing, tribes and families marked agreements with symbols. A carved line or pressed handprint carried meaning of promise. The mark represented living witness. Over time, signatures replaced symbols, yet purpose remained the same. To sign is to declare, "I stand by what I have written." This act unites voice, mind, and hand. It joins unseen world of thought with visible world of form.

Every system of governance understands this power. Councils, banks, and courts demand signature because it binds intention. Once signed, paper becomes evidence of will. That is why contracts, forms, and declarations all require it. Yet few realise that same principle empowers the individual. When you sign in peace, your signature carries authority equal to any institution. The question is not whose pen writes but whose conscience guides hand.

The seal of the living word carries both moral and lawful weight. Moral, because it represents truth within. Lawful, because it completes process of evidence. A letter without signature can be dismissed as draft or opinion. A letter signed clearly and dated stands as statement. It may be ignored, but it cannot be denied. Even silence from recipient recognises its existence.

To give strength to record, always sign in blue ink. Blue distinguishes original from copy. It symbolises life and creativity rather than bureaucracy. Black belongs to system, blue to living being. The colour itself has no magic; meaning lies in intention. By choosing blue, you remind yourself that you act from life, not from fiction.

Placement of signature also matters. Always sign at end of document, below final sentence. This indicates closure and completion. Write full name as you normally would, followed by phrase "a living man" or "a living woman." This separates natural being from artificial person created by registration. The system cannot claim ownership over name attached to life rather than corporation.

Some people add thumbprint in blue or red ink beside signature as personal seal. The print represents physical presence and uniqueness of being. It says, "No one else could have made this mark." Use of thumbprint is optional but meaningful. It carries ancient symbolism of blood, life, and authenticity.

Witnessing enhances power of signature. A witness confirms act of signing, not truth of content. Their role is simple: to observe and record that you signed freely and knowingly. Choose witness of sound mind and good reputation. They need not be official or legal professional. A friend, neighbour, or family member of honourable character is sufficient. Their signature beneath yours strengthens integrity of record.

When acting as witness for another, remember seriousness of role. You are not agreeing with document but affirming event. Write clearly, "Signed in my presence," followed by name, signature, and date. This small addition turns private act into verified occurrence. Law respects witness because it introduces third party of conscience.

The seal of the living word loses meaning when used carelessly. Never sign document without full understanding of content. Many fall into trap of signing under pressure. Councils and agencies rely on haste. They present forms requiring immediate signature, using authority to induce fear. True honour requires calm reflection. Read every word, question unclear terms, and sign only when conscience agrees. Silence and delay are lawful responses when peace of mind is uncertain.

Your signature is extension of your soul. Each one carries energy of moment it was made. Sign in anger, and paper holds vibration of conflict. Sign in peace, and record radiates calmness. Before signing, pause and breathe. Feel alignment between heart and words. When balance is present, proceed. This ritual connects physical action with spiritual intent.

The act of signing also represents acceptance of responsibility. Once name appears on document, it belongs to you. That is reason to write with care. Each word signed becomes part of your lawful story. Think of signature as final breath of sentence, sealing thought into eternity. Words written may fade, but name remains witness.

Institutions use signature to bind you to contracts. You can use same principle to bind them to truth. When sending notice or affidavit, request signature of responsible officer. Ask them to confirm by name and title that statements made in reply are true to best of their knowledge. Few will do so, for few wish to place conscience behind policy. Their refusal exposes difference between living honour and corporate evasion.

The seal of the living word also marks boundaries. Once you sign and serve document, matter moves from thought to law. You have spoken. Further repetition weakens record. Let signature end conversation until reply arrives. Trust power of written and signed word to stand on its own.

For long documents such as affidavits, initial each page at bottom corner. This confirms that all pages belong to same record. Number pages clearly. Sign only final page with full name and date. This simple practice prevents tampering or substitution. Law recognises completeness through sequence.

Keep separate notebook listing all documents you have signed, with date, title, and purpose. This ledger becomes index of your commitment. Reading it reminds you how often truth has spoken through your hand. It deepens respect for process. The more you treat signature as sacred act, the stronger its effect.

Avoid printing digital copies with pre-scanned signature for important documents. Mechanical reproduction lacks energy of real act. Use printed name only when document is clearly informal. For all lawful communication, use original ink. Living record requires living touch.

When serving documents that require confirmation from others, request that they sign receipt. This signature creates chain of accountability. Each link represents moment of truth. Whether or not they understand significance, the act binds them morally.

The next section will explore deeper symbolism of seal and oath, showing how word spoken or written in truth becomes unbreakable law of conscience. It will explain why systems fear oath of living being and how integrity behind word defines authority more than title or position.

Every mark that carries your name echoes through time. The system recognises this echo and uses it to maintain control. Yet the same law that binds through ignorance frees through awareness. When you understand sacred nature of word and signature, you reclaim authorship of life. The seal of living word turns tool of control into instrument of liberation.

The signature is not ownership; it is authorship. Ownership seeks possession, authorship expresses creation. When you sign in peace, you do not claim domination over others. You affirm presence within truth. This distinction transforms meaning of act. The state uses signature to enforce submission. The Sovereign uses it to declare responsibility. Both act under same principle of consent, but motive changes direction.

The oath completes this principle. To swear or affirm truth before witness joins voice to conscience. It means, "My word is enough because it comes from truth within me." This oath does not depend on religion or title. It depends on awareness of life. The living being who speaks truth under oath carries authority of nature itself.

Courts fear such oath because it bypasses their hierarchy. An oath made directly to truth leaves no room for manipulation. Once sworn, it binds more strongly than statute. For this reason, officials often avoid personal affirmation. They hide behind collective signatures such as "Legal Department." The absence of living name reveals absence of conscience. The system's weakness lies in its anonymity.

When you sign or affirm, you act as witness of creation. You testify that truth has entered world through you. This awareness removes need for external validation. The paper no longer seeks approval. It already holds life through your mark. Others may ignore or deny it, yet truth does not fade. It remains alive within record.

The seal of living word also protects against falsehood. If someone produces document with your name without consent, you can show difference. Each true signature carries unique rhythm and presence. No imitation can match energy of genuine act performed in peace. In conflict, calm comparison of handwriting and ink will expose fraud. Law always recognises authenticity when evidence is clear.

Never allow fear to dictate when or how you sign. Some refuse to sign anything, believing all signatures dangerous. This extreme position leads to paralysis. Signature itself is not trap; ignorance is. When you sign with full understanding and intention, you remain free. Only deceitful use of signature binds in dishonour.

Before signing any official document presented by authority, ask for complete copy of terms. Read slowly. If unclear, request explanation in writing. Never rely on verbal assurance. Once satisfied, sign with note stating, "Signed under protest and without prejudice to rights as living man or woman." This phrase reserves conscience while allowing process to continue. It transforms potential submission into lawful participation.

Your signature also interacts with energy of space. When you write in peaceful environment, ink flows evenly and handwriting appears balanced. When you write under tension, letters tighten and tilt. The page itself reveals emotional state. This is why careful preparation matters. Sit quietly before writing. Breathe deeply. Let calmness guide movement of hand. Each stroke becomes meditation of presence.

The seal of living word may extend beyond name. Some create personal emblem or motto representing principles they live by. When added discreetly near signature, it reinforces identity. Example: a simple symbol of balance or phrase such as "In peace and honour." These additions are not decoration but declaration. They remind both writer and reader of higher purpose behind record.

In times of confusion, reading your own signed documents restores confidence. Seeing name written in strength recalls moment of certainty. It reminds you that truth still stands. Each signature becomes milestone marking path of awareness. The archive of signed papers forms map of growth.

Witnessing also teaches humility. When you watch another declare truth and sign calmly, you feel weight of act. You sense sacredness of record. This shared experience strengthens trust within community of lawful living. Each witness becomes guardian of truth. Together they form network of accountability beyond control of system.

Some may attempt to question authority of your signature, arguing that it lacks legal status. They forget that law itself depends on signature of men and women who created it. Every statute, act, and decree bears names of those who believed in its words. Without signature, no law exists. Authority flows from living beings, not from ink. When you sign in truth, you stand equal with any legislator.

Integrity of word determines value of signature. The liar's mark is burden; the honest man's mark is shield. You can tell difference by effect it produces. Deceitful signature invites conflict, truthful one brings calm. The universe aligns with sincerity. It protects those who act in truth.

Over time, you will learn to sense when document deserves signature and when it does not. This intuition arises from practice, not fear. Trust feeling of resistance. If something feels wrong, do not sign until clarity returns. Law rewards caution. Rushing serves those who wish to exploit confusion.

After signing, always keep original or certified copy. Never hand over only version of document bearing your signature without duplicate. Retain evidence of every act. Your signature is valuable; treat it accordingly. Councils guard their seals carefully because they know power of mark. You must do same.

One day, your signature will appear on final declaration of life, such as will or testament. That moment will summarise all lessons learned. The peace with which you sign will reflect peace achieved through years of lawful living. Every earlier signature prepares you for that final affirmation of truth.

To understand deeper symbolism, reflect on phrase "word made flesh." It describes process by which idea becomes reality. In same way, signature turns invisible thought into visible proof. Each signed document is small act of creation. The universe records every act done in honour as contribution to order.

When truth flows through you and into record, you fulfil purpose of living law. You become bridge between unseen and seen, between conscience and form. Signature becomes sacred ritual marking unity of these worlds. Once understood, you will never treat act lightly again.

The next chapter will explore concept of time, silence, and acquiescence, showing how patience strengthens record and how the passage of time converts unrebutted truth into lawful standing. It will explain rhythm of law that moves not through force but through trust in time's quiet justice.

Chapter 7:
Time, Silence, and Acquiescence

Law moves through rhythm of time. Every notice, affidavit, and declaration gains strength not only from words written but from days that follow. Time is silent witness that confirms truth. The impatient man demands result; the wise man waits for law to mature. When you understand how time transforms silence into agreement, you unlock one of the oldest principles of justice.

In ancient societies, law was spoken before witnesses who marked passage of days with care. If no objection was made within set period, claim became fact. This practice reflected understanding that truth requires opportunity for challenge. Silence after fair notice equals consent. That simple idea survives in every legal system today. Councils, banks, and courts rely upon it constantly. They send letters, wait for silence, then act as if agreement exists. What few realise is that same principle protects the living being who acts in honour.

Time is neutral. It favours neither authority nor individual. It serves whoever respects it. The system uses deadlines to control. The Sovereign uses patience to liberate. Each notice you send includes condition of time. You offer period of reflection to recipient. If they reply, you continue dialogue. If they remain silent, you accept silence as confirmation that claim stands unrebutted. This is not arrogance; it is law.

Understanding acquiescence removes fear of silence. Most people panic when letters go unanswered. They mistake lack of response for uncertainty. In truth, silence speaks loudly. The council that fails to answer question within reasonable time admits weakness of position. Their authority depends on presumption. Your notice removes presumption by demanding proof. When proof does not come, silence becomes evidence.

To use time lawfully, you must first define it clearly. Each notice should specify exact period for reply. The common range is fourteen to twenty-one days, long enough for consideration, short enough to prevent delay. Always include statement such as, "Failure to reply within this period will be taken as confirmation of acceptance and agreement with terms herein." These words transform time into contract.

When deadline passes, record it calmly. Write short note in your journal: "Notice served on date. Reply due on date. No reply received." This simple entry becomes proof of process. Do not rush to send second notice immediately. Allow few extra days for delivery or internal delay. Patience reinforces fairness. When you finally write follow-up titled "Notice of Default," you act from balance, not frustration.

Silence is powerful because it cannot lie. Words can deceive; silence cannot. It reveals truth by absence. When official avoids direct answer, they confirm what they wish to hide. You learn more from what they do not say than from what they do. This awareness removes need for argument. Let their silence become confession.

Acquiescence means acceptance through inaction. It arises when opportunity to object passes unused. Law respects this because fairness demands closure. Endless waiting breeds confusion. When both sides have had chance to speak and one remains silent, matter ends. This closure allows life to move forward. The Sovereign honours same rule. When someone sends you notice, reply within reasonable time. If claim is false, rebut it clearly. If true, acknowledge it. This balance keeps flow of honour alive.

Time also cleanses emotion. During waiting period, mind settles. Anger fades, fear subsides, and truth becomes clearer. The silence between letters is not empty; it is field of reflection. Each day adds distance from conflict. That distance reveals perspective. By the time reply is due, you will know whether further action is needed or peace already achieved.

The system fears patience because patience cannot be manipulated. Bureaucracy thrives on urgency. It sends reminders marked "immediate action required" to provoke reaction. The Sovereign reads calmly, notes date, and files letter. Reaction gives power; reflection restores it. Once you master patience, their urgency loses hold.

Keep in mind that time has spiritual dimension. It is not mere counting of days but rhythm of truth revealing itself. When you act in honour and wait with peace, universe itself supports your record. Events align subtly. Opportunities appear, misunderstandings dissolve, and silence of others becomes clarity within you. Law mirrors this harmony. True justice unfolds naturally when forced impatience ceases.

To practise principle of time, maintain calendar dedicated to lawful matters. Mark each notice sent, date of service, and response due. Review weekly. This simple routine prevents oversight and builds confidence. Knowing that everything is tracked allows mind to rest. Anxiety thrives in uncertainty; organisation cures it.

Remember also that patience is not passivity. It is active trust. You continue living fully while waiting. You do not obsess over outcome. The letter has been sent, the record created, the silence unfolding. Interfering with process shows doubt. Faith in truth means allowing time to work.

The law of time operates within you as well. Each stage of awakening requires period of silence before understanding deepens. You read, reflect, and only later act. Rushing growth leads to error. The same pattern applies to record. Let each document breathe before moving to next. The gap between letters carries energy of transformation.

The next section will explore practical application of these principles, showing how to calculate reasonable timeframes, how to use follow-up notices correctly, and how to interpret different kinds of silence. It will also discuss moral responsibility that accompanies power of patience, reminding you that time given must always be fair and used in peace.

Time, silence, and acquiescence form the quiet machinery of law. They turn motion of life into record of agreement. To master them is to live without fear of delay or inaction. The man who understands time never feels urgency from others. He moves according to rhythm of truth, not pressure of letters. The system depends on people forgetting that time belongs to them.

A council may send demand marked with short deadline, suggesting disaster will follow if payment is not made. Yet law itself requires fairness. Any demand must allow reasonable opportunity to reply. You are entitled to equal time as claimant had to prepare their notice. This principle, called equity, protects balance between parties. Awareness of it frees you from intimidation.

In your own notices, fairness must remain central. The time you give must be reasonable. Fourteen days is common minimum, twenty-one preferred. Always choose period you can honour yourself. If you demand reply within short time and cannot respond equally fast, you act in contradiction. Honour requires consistency. Law respects those who apply same measure to others as they expect in return.

When time passes and silence remains, record gains maturity. The unrebutted notice becomes evidence of agreement. You need not celebrate or announce victory. Quietly note completion in your archive. Write short statement such as, "No reply received; matter closed through acquiescence." This keeps record factual and calm.

There are two kinds of silence: deliberate and unconscious. Deliberate silence is choice made by official who cannot answer truthfully. They hide behind procedure, knowing reply would expose error. Unconscious silence occurs when correspondence is lost or ignored through neglect. The wise man treats both with same patience. You cannot know which type applies, so act only after reasonable period. This patience protects honour even when others act carelessly.

Sometimes you will receive late reply after deadline. When this happens, acknowledge it politely. Do not reject automatically. Read carefully. If response resolves matter in peace, accept it. If it ignores your questions, remind sender that time for rebuttal has passed and record stands as written. This shows fairness and confidence. Law supports one who allows second chance but remains firm in truth.

Time also applies to your silence. When notice arrives from council, choose silence deliberately, not through fear. Ignoring letter in panic creates dishonour because silence was unearned. Choosing silence after clear communication expresses strength. The difference lies in intention. One runs from truth; the other stands within it.

There will be occasions when you must decide whether to write again or let matter rest. Listen to intuition. If peace exists, do not disturb it. Silence that follows understanding is closure. If confusion lingers, write short clarification, not full letter. Lawful communication is not endless conversation but series of precise steps ending in harmony.

Acquiescence is double-edged principle. It can serve truth or deceit. When used by system, it binds through ignorance. When used by Sovereign, it liberates through awareness. The same rule applies in both cases: silence equals agreement. The difference lies in consciousness of parties involved. To ensure fairness, you must always give full opportunity for reply. A notice that traps recipient through trickery dishonours both sides.

Patience also reveals deeper lesson. It teaches trust in order beyond human control. Time governs growth of plants, flow of rivers, and rise of stars. It governs truth with same precision. Every claim ripens in its own season. Rushing process disturbs balance. When you learn to move with rhythm of time, fear vanishes. You no longer demand immediate justice because you know justice already unfolding.

Practical discipline strengthens faith. Keep clear record of all timelines. Mark start and end dates in calendar. When tempted to act prematurely, look at dates. Seeing time written reminds you that process continues even while you rest. Each passing day adds invisible weight to your record. Silence of others becomes ally rather than enemy.

Do not confuse patience with resignation. Waiting does not mean surrendering rights. It means respecting sequence of law. Every stage of communication requires space for reflection. When you send notice, you plant seed. The soil of time must nurture it before fruit appears. Digging it up daily to check progress kills growth.

Silence can also be used strategically. In discussion with authority, pause before replying to question. This pause unsettles assumption. Officials expect immediate reaction. Your calm silence forces them to consider words carefully. It reminds them that you are not under their control. Silence creates gravity. It draws attention without noise.

Understanding these subtleties of silence gives confidence even in court or hearing. When question feels unfair or unclear, ask for clarification instead of rushing to answer. This controlled stillness turns pressure into strength. Law respects composure. The one who remains calm commands situation quietly.

Acquiescence operates beyond written record. In daily life, silence after kindness becomes appreciation. Silence after insult becomes forgiveness. Same principle flows through all interactions. Learning patience with others mirrors patience with law. Both teach compassion.

The final lesson of time is closure. When matter ends, let it end. Do not reopen old wounds through curiosity or pride. Once silence has served its purpose, move forward. Your energy belongs to present, not past. The archive keeps memory safe; you need not carry it in mind. Peace arises from ability to release.

Through mastery of time, silence, and acquiescence, you enter deeper relationship with truth. You stop chasing outcomes and start observing process. Life becomes series of measured acts rather than emotional reactions. Each letter, each waiting period, each moment of quiet reflection contributes to strength of record and serenity of spirit.

The next chapter will explore how private record becomes public awareness. It will show how truth written in peace eventually reaches others, not through argument but through quiet presence of evidence. You will learn how to share record responsibly without pride or fear, allowing truth to serve community through example.

Chapter 8:
From Private Record to Public Knowledge

Truth begins in private space. It grows quietly within man or woman who has chosen peace over fear. Yet truth does not remain hidden forever. When written and preserved with honour, it eventually touches world beyond its author. This movement from private record to public knowledge happens naturally, not by force. The living being who keeps faithful record becomes living example of law in action. The archive built in silence becomes beacon that guides others toward understanding.

Every authority seeks to control narrative. Councils and governments publish documents shaping public belief. They decide what appears official and what remains unseen. The private record challenges that monopoly. It stands outside system of permission. It says, "Truth does not need licence to exist." Once written, truth exists independently of recognition.

Moving from private record to public awareness requires care. Truth loses purity when shared for attention. It must never become performance. The purpose of sharing record is service, not pride. When motive is clean, truth travels safely. When motive is self-promotion, truth becomes distorted. The one who wishes to serve others through knowledge must first remain invisible servant of truth itself.

Begin by asking why you wish to share your record. Is it to prove others wrong, or to show that peace works? If reason is peace, proceed. If reason is ego, wait until clarity returns. Lawful living requires honesty about intention. The moment motive shifts from truth to victory, energy of record changes. The world feels difference even if words remain same.

When record is shared correctly, it teaches without argument. A friend may ask how you handled certain matter with council. You can show them your letters, notices, and replies. They see order, calmness, and respect. You explain process, not outcome. This approach spreads knowledge without confrontation. It invites reflection instead of resistance.

Public awareness often begins quietly. One person reads your letters and decides to write their own. Another learns value of record through observation. Gradually, community of honour grows. None need title or leader. Each acts from conscience, guided by same principles. Private truth becomes collective practice. This is how peaceful revolution begins.

The shift from private to public also teaches responsibility. Once others look to your example, you carry duty to remain consistent. Words and actions must align. Hypocrisy destroys credibility faster than error. If you make mistake, admit it openly. Correction strengthens trust. The honest man who learns in public helps more than proud man who pretends perfection.

Do not rush to publish every document online. The internet invites distortion. Once shared, letters lose context and can be misused. Before releasing any material, remove personal details and ensure content cannot be interpreted as instruction or legal advice. Emphasise always that record is educational example, not template for others to copy blindly. Freedom grows through understanding, not imitation.

Sometimes truth travels further than expected. Letter written in peace may reach hands of official who reads it privately and begins to question system. Such moments happen quietly, unseen by you. That is how truth works. It moves through conscience of others without need for applause. Trust unseen ripple of your actions. The living record changes world by example, not by campaign.

Public knowledge differs from publicity. Publicity seeks reaction; knowledge seeks awareness. When your record becomes known, remain detached. You are not owner of truth; you are custodian. Many will interpret your work according to their own understanding. Some will praise, others will criticise. Accept both with calmness. Praise and blame belong to same illusion. Truth remains unchanged.

When speaking publicly about record, use language of experience, not instruction. Say, "In my case I found that writing calmly brought peace," rather than, "You should write this way." The first inspires reflection; the second provokes defence. The purpose is not to convert but to awaken curiosity.

Public knowledge also brings challenge. Those invested in system may feel threatened by new understanding. They may question your authority or mock your belief. Respond with kindness. Mockery reveals fear. Those who defend illusion of power sense its weakness. Your calmness exposes their insecurity. Silence often answers better than words.

To bring record into public domain effectively, consider sharing principles rather than documents. Write short essays explaining ideas behind your actions. Teach concept of honour, consent, and record keeping. Use examples without revealing personal correspondence. This preserves privacy while spreading wisdom. The message becomes timeless because it focuses on principle, not personality.

Another way to share truth is through conversation. Speak quietly with those who show interest. Share experiences face to face. In direct dialogue, energy of peace communicates more strongly than words. Eye contact and tone carry sincerity that written page cannot. Many awaken through feeling presence of calmness rather than reading complex explanations.

Remember that true public record is not loud. It exists wherever man or woman lives lawfully. Every time you act with honour in daily life, you add to invisible archive of humanity. Each peaceful exchange, each act of integrity, each written truth contributes to collective memory of freedom. You may never see result, yet it grows silently.

When your record becomes known to community, protect it from distortion by keeping master copies secure. Provide copies only when necessary and always mark them "for study and education." This simple phrase clarifies intent. It separates knowledge from advice and prevents misuse. Law respects clarity of purpose.

As awareness spreads, some may ask you to teach. Accept only if you feel peace in doing so. Teaching requires humility. You must remain student even while explaining. Never present yourself as authority over others. The Sovereign recognises no master except truth. Teaching is service, not command.

The growth of public knowledge brings paradox. The more people understand lawful living, the less they need to speak of it. Once peace becomes habit, explanation fades. The world changes quietly because men and women stop reacting to illusion of power. They simply live differently. The record becomes culture rather than counteraction.

This transformation begins with one archive. Every private folder is seed of future understanding. When many keep records with honesty, collective memory shifts. Society that values written truth cannot be deceived easily. Lies wither in light of evidence. The system thrives on forgetfulness; record restores memory.

Eventually, public institutions themselves may adopt principles of honour. Councils may begin answering notices respectfully. Courts may acknowledge affidavits without prejudice. Such changes appear slow but inevitable. Law evolves when enough individuals embody it. Reform begins not in office but in heart.

The next section will explore how to share record while maintaining peace and humility. It will discuss dangers of pride, temptation of recognition, and importance of remaining servant of truth even when others call you teacher. The path from private to public ends not with fame but with deeper quietness.

When truth leaves private room of conscience and steps into public world, new tests appear. You will face curiosity, challenge, and admiration in equal measure. Each reaction invites you to practise peace. The task is no longer to prove record correct but to remain calm while others discover their own understanding. Public knowledge is mirror reflecting collective state of awareness. How you respond to that reflection determines whether truth continues to grow or becomes entangled in conflict.

Sharing record responsibly begins with humility. You are not messenger of final truth but student who has chosen to share what has been learned. Speak as one voice among many, not as authority. This attitude keeps communication balanced. It prevents creation of hierarchy where none belongs. Lawful knowledge belongs to all living beings equally.

When explaining concepts to others, simplify language. Avoid technical terms unless necessary. Many people fear law because they associate it with complexity. Show that truth is simple and accessible. Use examples drawn from daily life. Describe record keeping as act of respect, not rebellion. Help them see that peace begins with clarity, not confrontation.

Be careful when others praise you. Compliments can feel pleasant but may inflate pride. Pride weakens connection to truth. Accept kind words with gratitude but remember that honour belongs to process, not person. The same principle applies to criticism. When attacked or mocked, remain steady. Criticism tests patience. Respond only when response serves peace. Most of the time silence is answer.

Avoid forming groups or organisations that claim exclusive understanding. The moment structure appears, politics follows. Keep exchange of knowledge open and informal. Encourage others to think for themselves and adapt principles to their own conscience. Freedom loses meaning when bound by membership. True community forms naturally through mutual respect, not through oath or registration.

When you speak publicly or write essays, include clear reminder that your material is educational and philosophical. This distinction protects both you and audience. People often seek quick remedy or shortcut to avoid responsibility. Teach them that lawful living is journey of patience. Record is tool of conscience, not escape from obligation.

As awareness spreads, temptation arises to seek recognition. Some begin to measure success by number of followers or views. This path leads away from honour. The measure of truth is not applause but peace. If your life remains calm while others learn from you, then teaching has succeeded. Fame serves ego; service serves truth. Choose service.

Sharing record also demands discernment. Not every listener is ready for full understanding. Some approach with curiosity, others with hostility. Learn to sense difference. With the sincere, share freely. With the hostile, remain brief and polite. The purpose of dialogue is harmony, not victory.

When record enters public sphere, it invites scrutiny. Welcome honest questions. Transparency strengthens credibility. If error is found, correct it without hesitation. Correction shows maturity. The world respects those who refine their understanding openly. Concealment of mistake harms both teacher and student.

You may notice that public awareness grows unevenly. Some grasp principles quickly, others struggle. Do not force pace. Each mind unfolds in its own time, just as each notice matures through silence. Patience in teaching mirrors patience in correspondence. The one who allows others space to learn embodies same law they speak of.

Never turn lawful knowledge into argument. Debate wastes energy. Instead, ask questions that encourage reflection. For example, if someone insists that government power is absolute, ask, "Where does that power begin?" or "Who gave consent?" These questions invite thought without conflict. They plant seeds of awareness that may bloom later.

When speaking about your record, emphasise experience rather than theory. Share what you have lived, not what you have heard. Personal example carries more power than abstract idea. It proves that honour works in real world. The listener sees transformation rather than hears claim.

Protect your record from being used for harm. Some may copy documents or phrases and twist them into aggression. To prevent this, always attach statement clarifying that record is for peaceful study only. This boundary reminds others that truth without honour becomes distortion.

The movement from private to public also reveals strength of your inner peace. Exposure tests ego. Public reaction mirrors unfinished lessons. If anger arises when misunderstood, pause and reflect. The world is teacher showing where attachment remains. Each misunderstanding is opportunity to deepen calmness.

Be selective with time and energy. Not every conversation deserves response. Choose engagements that uplift. Withdraw from endless argument. Silence can teach more than words when delivered with respect. Those who truly seek understanding will return quietly later.

As more people adopt practice of record keeping, collective behaviour changes. Officials notice difference in tone of correspondence they receive. Letters become clear, respectful, and precise. Fear diminishes. Bureaucracy softens under weight of calm evidence. Gradual reform begins, not through protest but through dignity.

Your record may one day be requested as example by others wishing to learn. Share it if you feel peace, but always remove personal details. Teach method, not identity. The process belongs to all, the story remains yours. This protects both privacy and integrity of lesson.

Public awareness also brings challenge of imitation without understanding. Some copy language of honour but keep spirit of conflict. Their words sound lawful yet feel harsh. This happens when form is taken without substance. If you see this, do not condemn. Remember your own beginning when clarity was still forming. Offer gentle guidance if invited; otherwise remain silent.

As truth spreads, gratitude becomes essential practice. Thank those who question you, for they strengthen precision. Thank those who misunderstand, for they reveal where patience grows. Thank those who listen, for they carry message forward. Gratitude keeps ego from poisoning service.

Eventually, role of teacher fades. Others become teachers themselves, and your work continues through them. This is natural progression of truth. The river does not hold water; it lets water flow. In same way, you let knowledge move freely. The less you control it, the purer it remains.

The true purpose of sharing record is to remind humanity that law and conscience are one. The written word was never meant to divide but to unite through clarity. Each living being who writes in peace contributes to restoration of that unity. Public knowledge then becomes not threat to authority but return to balance.

When you witness others awakening through your example, remain quiet inside. Joy may rise, but let it stay private. The moment you claim credit, flow of truth slows. Continue living as before, writing letters when necessary, keeping record, and teaching only when asked. The greatest influence is unseen.

In time, the idea of private and public dissolves entirely. All record becomes living law expressed through every action. People no longer separate conscience from communication. Honour becomes culture. Society that lives this way requires few statutes. Each man and woman becomes own lawmaker guided by truth.

The next chapter will show how record must be used ethically, never as weapon. It will explain difference between defence and attack, showing why honour forbids aggression even when provoked. The archive of truth protects but never harms. Peace remains greatest proof of sovereignty.

Chapter 9:
Record as Shield, Not Sword

The written record is tool of peace. It protects truth but must never be used to harm. Many who first learn principles of lawful communication make mistake of treating record as weapon. They seek victory instead of understanding. This error destroys honour and invites conflict. The record's power lies in its ability to defend, not to attack. It serves as shield that preserves dignity of both writer and recipient.

To use record lawfully, motive must remain pure. The purpose of every notice, affidavit, and declaration is to restore balance, not to gain advantage. The living being who writes from anger creates vibration of hostility that weakens evidence. Law responds to energy behind words as much as to words themselves. A letter written in peace holds greater strength than a demand filled with rage. The universe recognises tone before it considers content.

A shield protects without striking. It absorbs impact of aggression and turns it into stillness. In same way, record absorbs tension of dispute. When council sends threat or demand, you respond with clarity. You do not mirror aggression. You reply with measured language that returns responsibility to sender. This is lawful self-defence. It prevents escalation while establishing boundary. The system expects fear. When met with calmness, it loses control.

There is deep morality behind using record as defence. Lawful communication reflects natural law, which forbids harm. The maxim remains simple: cause no injury, loss, or deceit. Writing with intention to punish or humiliate breaks this law. Writing with intention to reveal truth honours it. The difference lies in motive. The one who writes to correct stands in grace. The one who writes to conquer falls into same trap as oppressor.

When learning art of notice and affidavit, avoid temptation to overwhelm with quantity. Some believe long letters filled with complex language show authority. In truth, simplicity shows mastery. The more direct your letter, the stronger its impact. A single paragraph written with honesty carries more weight than ten pages written in pride. Record is not competition. It is conversation with truth.

Aggression in writing reveals fear. The person who attacks through letters feels uncertain of standing. True authority has no need to shout. Calmness is proof of confidence. Officials often react with confusion when they receive peaceful letters because system trains them to face anger. They expect confrontation. When confronted by gentleness, they see reflection of conscience. Some even soften unconsciously.

Using record as shield means responding only when necessary. Not every provocation deserves reply. Silence can defend more effectively than words. The wise man distinguishes between attack that requires clarification and noise that seeks attention. Respond to first with peace, ignore second completely. Reaction feeds conflict. Restraint ends it.

There are moments when false accusation or threat arrives. The instinct to defend immediately is strong. Yet even in such moment, pause before writing. Gather facts. Read letter again next day. Often emotion fades, and response becomes clearer. Acting too quickly turns shield into sword. Patience sharpens precision.

If you must write defence, keep tone factual. Example: "I have received your letter dated this day. I do not accept claim contained within. Please provide proof of contract signed by both parties." Such statement holds strength without hostility. It deflects attack by returning burden of proof. The record stands between you and aggression, absorbing impact without reflecting harm.

Remember that officials are human beings. Many act from habit rather than malice. Treat them with courtesy even when they err. A polite letter addressed to their conscience may reach deeper than angry demand. Some have never been spoken to with respect. Your tone may awaken memory of their own honour.

Never use lawful knowledge to intimidate or mock others. Wisdom is privilege that carries duty. The one who wields truth to belittle another turns blessing into curse. Education means service. Teach only through example. When others feel safe in your presence, they listen. When they feel judged, they resist.

Record as shield also protects mind. Writing transforms emotion into clarity. When faced with confusion or fear, putting thoughts on paper restores order. Even if letter is never sent, act of writing brings peace. The page becomes silent counsellor. Law begins within; record merely mirrors it.

If dispute continues despite peaceful notices, maintain same tone throughout. Consistency proves sincerity. Eventually pattern of honour becomes undeniable. The aggressor's letters grow harsher; yours remain calm. Anyone reviewing later will see difference clearly. Law favours side that remained in honour.

Keep copies of all correspondence as evidence of patience. When conflict ends, read through letters again. You will see how restraint prevented escalation. The archive becomes teacher showing power of quiet defence. Over time, confidence in process replaces need for aggression entirely.

The shield also represents boundary of responsibility. You protect what is yours but do not control what belongs to others. Once you have written truth and allowed time for reply, outcome lies beyond your power. Worrying or chasing result wastes energy. The shield does not chase arrows; it blocks them.

Some misunderstand lawful defence as weakness. They believe that peace means surrender. This is false. Peace requires greater strength than war. It demands control over ego and patience under pressure. The one who stands calmly before aggression demonstrates mastery of self. Law recognises this mastery even when world does not.

Using record as shield also prevents harm to innocent observers. Anger expressed through letters spreads negativity. Clerks reading them feel tension, which infects office atmosphere. Peaceful letters have opposite effect. They introduce calmness into environment built on stress. You become quiet reformer without knowing it.

There is also strategic wisdom in peaceful communication. When matter escalates to review or hearing, your correspondence will be examined. Letters filled with threats discredit your position. Letters written with respect win sympathy. Even officials who disagree with your beliefs cannot deny grace of your conduct.

Record as shield is ultimate expression of lawful living. It demonstrates belief in justice without need for force. It trusts that truth, once written, will protect itself. The sword demands attention. The shield works silently. Over time, silence achieves what noise cannot.

The next section will expand on this principle, showing how defence transforms into healing, how forgiveness strengthens record, and how true victory comes through peace that follows resolution rather than defeat of opponent.

The man or woman who has learned to use record as shield discovers freedom beyond conflict. Peace becomes constant companion, not because world grows gentle but because reaction has ended. When you refuse to fight yet continue to stand, others lose control over your spirit. That is strength the system cannot understand. It depends on resistance for survival. The moment you stop resisting and start recording, its power dissolves.

The shield teaches restraint. Every act of defence contains opportunity for forgiveness. When you forgive, energy of attack returns to sender. The record reflects forgiveness through calm language. A letter that begins, "I wish to resolve this in peace," carries vibration that disarms hostility. It does not yield truth but removes tension. Many officials respond kindly when met with respect. They expect anger; they receive courtesy. This shift breaks chain of conflict that binds system to fear.

The one who fights with sword always meets another sword. The one who holds shield meets silence. Over time, silence wears down aggression. Law operates by same principle. The claimant who cannot prove loses claim. The defendant who remains calm allows time to expose weakness. Fighting delays peace; patience reveals it.

When you write, think not of victory but of closure. The purpose of defence is not to win argument but to restore balance. Once balance returns, cease communication. Endless defence becomes offence in disguise. Let stillness finish work that words began.

You will encounter people who misunderstand your calmness. They will call it avoidance or cowardice. Smile inwardly. They mistake noise for strength. True courage lies in patience. The man who restrains anger achieves victory unseen by crowd. His conscience remains clean.

Each written record carries echo of writer's state. Words used as weapon pierce only for moment; words written in peace endure for generations. Many sacred texts survive because they were written in calm awareness. That same energy can infuse your letters when intention is pure. Those who read them in future will feel balance within sentences. Even officials may sense it unconsciously.

Using record as shield also protects heart. Aggression drains energy, peace restores it. Each time you respond with calmness, you strengthen inner discipline. This training extends beyond law into daily life. Arguments at work, misunderstandings with neighbours, family disputes—all dissolve faster when treated with same principle. Lawful living becomes way of being, not collection of documents.

To maintain shield effectively, build rhythm of peace. Before replying to any letter, spend moment in silence. Breathe slowly. Ask whether response serves truth or ego. If ego speaks, wait. When truth speaks, write. This pause saves many mistakes. The mind cooled by silence writes with precision.

Forgiveness within record does not mean forgetting injustice. It means releasing need for revenge. You still demand proof, but you do so without hatred. This distinction transforms energy. The system cannot engage when opponent refuses hostility. Forgiveness removes fuel from fire. It leaves only light of truth.

A good example of shield in practice is notice written after repeated demands. Instead of angry complaint, you write: "I have previously asked for proof of claim. None has been received. Until such proof is provided, matter is considered settled in peace." This statement ends dispute with dignity. It invites response without aggression. Silence that follows becomes evidence of resolution.

Sometimes shield requires movement rather than stillness. If matter escalates to hearing or review, attend calmly. Bring copies of correspondence. Speak briefly and respectfully. Present facts without opinion. The one who attacks themselves appears unreasonable. You need only point to record. Law speaks through evidence, not emotion.

Your physical presence also communicates peace. Tone of voice, posture, and eye contact reinforce written record. Those trained to intimidate find it difficult to confront calmness. They rely on reaction. When none appears, they lose script. Many disputes resolve simply because one side remains tranquil.

Peaceful defence creates healing beyond dispute. Officials touched by your calmness may begin questioning their own role. Some quietly change behaviour without admitting it. Others carry memory of honour into next interaction. Each moment of restraint contributes to slow reform of culture.

To live this way requires daily practice. Keep journal describing situations where you used shield successfully. Record feelings before and after each exchange. Over time, you will see transformation of temperament. What once caused anger will soon cause only compassion. This inner change is true measure of sovereignty.

The shield also symbolises trust in natural order. You believe truth defends itself through law of cause and effect. Every action carries consequence. You need not control outcome because justice operates through time. When record stands in peace, universe aligns events to protect it. Trust this process even when results seem delayed.

Those who continue to attack after repeated notices reveal their fear of truth. Pity them, for they know not what they do. Their aggression harms only themselves. Respond once more with courtesy, then remain silent. The archive will show difference between honour and hostility. Law always sides with balance.

Teach others to use record this way. Explain that lawful defence is act of love, not defiance. Encourage them to write clearly, wait patiently, and forgive freely. When many live by these principles, collective shield forms around community. Violence fades because there is nothing left to fight.

The true warrior of law carries pen, not sword. His battle is with ignorance, his weapon is understanding, his victory is peace. He does not seek followers, only fellow travellers. Each letter written in honour becomes silent prayer for harmony.

Remember always that shield is symbol, not object. It represents state of mind that refuses to harm. Once you master this state, even spoken words become protection. Presence alone dissolves tension. People sense peace and cannot fight it.

When dispute ends, thank both parties within heart. Thank opponent for teaching patience. Thank yourself for remaining calm. Gratitude completes cycle of defence. It transforms conflict into wisdom. The one who lives this way no longer fears attack because every attack becomes lesson.

The chapter of shield ends with realisation that lawful living is not strategy but harmony. The record you build is reflection of that harmony. It protects not because of clever words but because of energy of truth within them. The sword seeks control; the shield trusts order.

The next chapter will explore how the record itself establishes lawful standing. It will show how consistent documentation of honour transforms private communication into recognised authority, and why standing arises from action rather than title.

Chapter 10: The Record of Standing

Standing is the quiet strength of lawful life. It is invisible yet undeniable. It cannot be granted by authority or taken by decree. It is earned through consistency of action and clarity of record. The man or woman who stands in truth becomes unshakable not because system recognises them but because conscience does. The record is outward proof of that inner reality.

In law, standing means right to be heard. Without it, claim or defence fails before it begins. Courts require proof of interest, evidence of harm, and connection to matter. These are external reflections of deeper principle. The living being gains standing not through forms or titles but through integrity. Every letter written, every affidavit signed, every moment of patience builds unseen foundation beneath words.

The system treats people as subjects. It assumes they act through corporate identity created by registration. The Sovereign corrects that presumption through record. Each document written in honour withdraws consent from fiction and replaces it with presence of life. Over time, pattern of truth emerges. Officials who read such correspondence recognise authenticity even if they cannot admit it publicly. Standing becomes obvious through tone, structure, and sincerity.

True standing begins when you realise that authority outside yourself depends on belief. Institutions hold power because people act as if they do. When you stop acting from fear and begin acting from awareness, illusion fades. The record confirms shift. Letters once written in panic now speak with peace. Demands become questions, questions become statements, and statements become declarations. The evolution of your writing mirrors evolution of your being.

To maintain standing, every act must align with truth. Contradiction weakens foundation. You cannot write notice demanding honour then act dishonourably in daily life. Lawful living is not divided between paper and person. It is single expression of integrity. When word and deed unite, standing becomes permanent.

The record also protects you from accusation of inconsistency. In dispute, officials may claim you changed position. The archive proves otherwise. Chronological order of letters shows progression of logic and fairness. Each document supports previous one like stones in wall. Anyone reviewing can trace clear path of honour. This visual proof of coherence gives authority to voice that speaks from peace.

There is difference between standing claimed and standing demonstrated. Many declare sovereignty loudly but cannot support claim with evidence of honour. Their words ring hollow because no record exists. The true Sovereign rarely declares anything. Their conduct speaks louder than slogans. The archive becomes their witness. Each affidavit, notice, and declaration stands as testimony to living law within them.

To cultivate record of standing, focus on quality, not quantity. Write only when necessary. Each letter should add clarity, not clutter. Redundancy confuses message. The fewer words you use, the more weight they carry. Precision reflects mastery. Law respects simplicity because truth needs no decoration.

Standing also requires knowledge of limits. The living man or woman does not seek control over others. They exercise authority only over their own affairs. Demanding obedience from institutions contradicts principle of freedom. The goal is not to rule but to be left in peace. The record demonstrates this by tone of humility. Each notice says, "I act in honour and seek resolution," not, "I command compliance."

Consistency of tone establishes credibility. Officials may disagree with philosophy but respect steadiness. When your letters always begin with peace and end with courtesy, you build reputation that outlasts argument. Over time, even those who resist your message treat you differently. They sense you will not be provoked. Standing commands respect silently.

The living being with standing acts from awareness of responsibility. Freedom without discipline leads to chaos. Standing without accountability becomes arrogance. Record balances both. It reminds you of promises made through written word. When you sign affidavit, you accept duty to live by it. Breaking oath weakens not only record but character. Honour grows through keeping word even when inconvenient.

The power of standing comes from stillness. It does not shout or demand recognition. It waits. In stillness, truth gathers weight. Like stone in river, it remains unmoved while water of noise flows around. Those who rush eventually tire; those who stand remain. The archive of correspondence reflects this endurance. Its pages bear marks of time yet remain intact.

Standing also influences community. People feel safe around those who live by principle. Your calm presence encourages others to act honourably. Without preaching, you become example. This quiet influence reforms society more effectively than protest. The strongest leaders rarely claim leadership. They serve truth and let truth lead.

To test your standing, ask whether your actions align with maxims you affirm. Do you cause no harm, no loss, no deceit? Do you speak truth even when inconvenient? Do you respect right of others to live free? If answer is yes, standing exists already. Paper merely records it.

Officials may challenge your standing by questioning authority behind documents. Respond calmly. Authority does not come from statute; it comes from life itself. The ability to write, think, and sign in peace is authority. Law exists because living beings speak truth. Without them, there would be no justice. This understanding removes need for external approval.

When you act from true standing, fear of error fades. You no longer worry about perfect phrasing or formatting. Spirit behind word carries message. Even if structure is simple, intention is clear. Law recognises sincerity. The court of conscience never rejects honest submission.

The next section will explore how standing interacts with evidence, how presumption yields to proof, and how the living record transforms silence into acknowledgement. You will learn how clarity of standing turns every unanswered notice into pillar of lawful authority built upon truth and patience.

Standing grows through evidence, not proclamation. The difference between belief and proof lies in written record. When you act honourably and document process, every unanswered notice, every affidavit of truth, and every declaration of peace becomes layer of foundation beneath your feet. You no longer rely on argument. Your life becomes its own evidence.

Presumption is the system's weapon. It fills silence with assumption. It claims authority where none has been granted, ownership where none exists, and agreement where none was given. The private record removes this illusion. Each written notice rebuts presumption calmly and permanently. Each affidavit of truth replaces assumption with fact. Over time, pattern of unrebutted communication creates unshakeable ground. That ground is your standing.

When you possess standing, tone of life changes. You stop asking for permission. You speak from awareness, not from fear. Every letter begins with confidence that truth defends itself. You no longer seek recognition from officials. Instead, you offer clarity. The difference between request and statement defines shift from weakness to strength.

Evidence of standing emerges naturally through sequence of correspondence. A single letter may not persuade anyone. Twelve letters written over months, each consistent in tone and purpose, reveal something deeper. They show persistence, fairness, and calmness. Even most sceptical observer sees pattern. Standing is visible through behaviour.

The power of standing also comes from silence that follows honourable action. When your notices receive no reply, system's quietness becomes testimony. Law recognises that silence, after opportunity to answer, equals acceptance. This is not manipulation. It is balance. You gave chance for response; it was not taken. Truth therefore stands unopposed.

Presumption collapses before clear evidence. The official who receives several letters, each polite and precise, cannot easily claim ignorance. They may ignore for a time, but record remains. If later challenged, you can show path of honour. The difference between you and them becomes obvious. You sought peace through process; they avoided it. Law respects side that acted in good faith.

To preserve standing, maintain purity of process. Do not exaggerate claims or attach threats. Simplicity speaks louder. For example, "I require proof of contract between living man and corporate body," is stronger than long paragraph filled with accusations. The first invites reply; the second provokes defence. True authority never hides behind noise.

Confidence in standing removes temptation to argue. The man without foundation shouts to be heard. The one with record speaks quietly because proof already exists. Argument ends where evidence begins. Every notice served, every affidavit signed, and every silence recorded becomes stone in structure of truth. You need not add decoration; structure stands by itself.

The record of standing also transforms relationships. Friends, colleagues, and family begin to sense change. Your speech becomes measured, your movements calm. You no longer react to threats or demands in same way. This inner stability draws respect even from those who disagree. They recognise strength of someone who lives by principle rather than fear.

Standing demands humility as well as strength. It is not certificate or status. It is way of living. Pride corrupts it quickly. The moment you begin to boast of sovereignty, standing diminishes. The law of balance ensures that truth remains linked to humility. You cannot dominate others and remain free. The living man or woman of honour walks quietly, carrying authority that requires no announcement.

Your standing also influences how others respond. When you write or speak from peace, you trigger recognition within conscience of recipient. Even officials trained to enforce policy feel subtle shift. They sense you cannot be coerced easily. That awareness changes tone of future correspondence. The system adapts to energy it meets. When met with chaos, it grows rigid. When met with peace, it relaxes.

To strengthen standing, align personal life with same discipline you apply to record. Keep promises, arrive on time, pay agreed debts, and speak honestly. Each act reinforces truth that record represents. Hypocrisy weakens energy behind words. Integrity in daily life charges documents with unseen power.

There may come moment when your record is questioned by authority seeking evidence of legitimacy. Remain calm. Produce archive showing sequence of notices, proof of service, and absence of rebuttal. Present it respectfully. You do not need to convince; record speaks for itself. Truth delivered in silence carries more weight than loud argument.

The one with standing no longer fears law because they understand origin of law. It arises from conscience. Every statute, rule, or order is attempt to imitate moral law. When conscience and record align, external laws lose power to intimidate. You live under higher jurisdiction of truth. This is not rebellion; it is restoration of natural balance.

Your standing is tested whenever authority demands compliance without proof. These moments reveal whether foundation is real or imagined. If fear returns, review archive. Read old letters. Remember how many times peace has defended you. Confidence grows through memory of past honour. The record itself becomes teacher reminding you that truth never fails.

Standing also connects to community. The individual who keeps record in peace strengthens collective conscience. Each man or woman who stands quietly in truth adds to invisible network of honour. Together they form moral foundation of society. No revolution required, only consistency. Lawful culture emerges when enough individuals live lawfully.

Do not expect public acknowledgement. The world rarely celebrates quiet strength. Recognition comes in subtler ways: fewer letters of demand, gentler tone from officials, smoother interactions. These signs confirm that system has recognised energy of peace even if it cannot name it. The record works silently behind scenes.

In time, standing becomes second nature. You no longer think of law as separate realm. It flows through ordinary acts. The same care you use in writing notice appears in conversation, work, and family life. You begin to live as constant witness of truth. That state is highest form of freedom.

The next chapter will explore concept of presumption and proof in greater depth. It will show how system builds illusion of authority through assumption, and how clear, consistent record replaces that illusion with evidence. You will learn how every unanswered question, every silence, and every affidavit forms chain of truth that no fiction can break.

Chapter 11:
Presumption and Proof

Law functions on presumption until proof replaces it. Every statute, claim, and demand made by authority begins with assumption. The system presumes you consent, presume you owe, and presume you agree. These presumptions operate silently beneath surface of communication. Most people live under them without realising. The private record exists to replace assumption with truth. Proof dissolves fiction as light dissolves darkness.

Presumption arises because law cannot act without foundation. To manage millions of people, governments must rely on general rules. They assume certain things true unless someone challenges. For example, they presume you are legal person attached to national register. They presume letters sent to address apply to you. They presume silence equals consent. These presumptions hold power only because they remain unrebutted.

Proof, on other hand, is specific. It does not rely on assumption. It stands on evidence. The living being who writes notices and affidavits operates within realm of proof. Each written document serves as beacon of clarity among ocean of presumption. It says, "I do not live by assumption. I live by truth that can be shown."

The struggle between presumption and proof shapes every interaction between individual and institution. The system sends notice claiming authority. The Sovereign replies asking for proof of claim. The system often remains silent because it cannot provide lawful evidence. Its power depends on compliance, not on truth. The moment you demand proof, illusion trembles.

To challenge presumption lawfully, you must act with precision. Do not attack or accuse. Simply request evidence. For example, when council sends demand for payment, reply with calm question: "Please provide proof of contract between you and living man." This shifts burden of proof. You have not refused; you have asked for verification. In law, refusal may create dishonour. Request for proof keeps you within honour.

Each unanswered request weakens presumption further. Silence from authority is admission that no proof exists. The longer silence continues, the stronger your record becomes. Eventually, unrebutted notices transform into lawful evidence that presumption has been overturned. Law respects sequence. Each step taken correctly replaces fiction with fact.

Understanding difference between presumption and proof changes how you see world. Most fear authority because they mistake assumption for evidence. They believe letter from council or order from court carries unchallengeable truth. In reality, it carries presumption of consent. Once consent is questioned, assumption collapses. The system cannot force belief; it can only request participation.

Proof requires clarity of communication. Your notices must be factual, not emotional. Each question must be specific. Vague or hostile letters allow recipient to ignore. Example: "Prove your authority to act under law" is too broad. Better: "Please provide copy of oath of office showing your lawful authority to enforce this demand." Specific request exposes gap between claim and evidence.

Record of unrebutted notices becomes collection of proofs. Over time, pattern of silence forms testimony stronger than words. Anyone reviewing correspondence will see clear chain of fairness. You asked reasonable questions; they did not answer. Law recognises this as fulfilment of duty to seek truth.

Presumption also operates internally. Many people assume they are powerless. They presume authority lies outside themselves. This mental habit sustains external control. When you build private record, you challenge inner presumption. You prove to yourself that conscience governs life. Each successful act of honour confirms that belief. Confidence replaces doubt.

Be aware that system rarely admits defeat. Even when proof is lacking, it continues acting under presumption of authority. This persistence does not negate truth. It merely shows inertia of bureaucracy. Do not take continued letters as evidence of correctness. They are repetition of old assumption. Reply once more with same calm question. Consistency is stronger than argument.

Proof and presumption also shape relationships between individuals. Misunderstandings often arise because people assume intent instead of asking. The discipline of lawful communication teaches you to verify before reacting. This habit extends beyond law into daily life. You stop presuming motives of others and begin seeking clarity. Peace grows naturally from honesty.

To master art of proof, keep evidence pure. Never falsify or exaggerate. Truth needs no embellishment. If you cannot prove claim, admit uncertainty. Law respects honesty more than confidence. The man who admits "I do not know" stands higher than one who insists on false certainty. Proof without integrity becomes manipulation.

The act of signing affidavit is highest form of proof because it binds conscience. Once sworn, it cannot be denied without counter affidavit. That is why institutions avoid responding directly to sworn testimony. They fear moral accountability. When you write affidavit of truth, you move from realm of opinion into realm of evidence. The silence that follows becomes proof of acceptance.

To live lawfully is to replace presumption with knowledge. Each step of awareness erases illusion. You no longer presume that system protects you; you know you protect yourself through honour. You no longer presume that silence means defeat; you know silence confirms truth. Every experience becomes classroom for understanding law of cause and effect.

The next section will examine practical ways to identify and dismantle presumptions in communication. It will show how to phrase questions that expose assumption, how to record silence as proof, and how to remain patient while truth unfolds through process of time.

Every presumption can be challenged, but only through clarity. Anger cannot defeat assumption; precision can. The mind that reacts strengthens illusion. The mind that questions dissolves it. The art of rebutting presumption lies in steady patience and simple truth expressed through writing. Each word becomes instrument of light uncovering what darkness hides.

To begin, learn to recognise common presumptions in communication. The first is presumption of personhood. Authorities presume you act as legal entity created by registration. They address letters to name written in capital letters. The private record distinguishes between that title and living being who answers with clarity. You never deny existence of name, for that would appear foolish, but you correct misunderstanding. You write, "I, a living man, am not sure to whom this notice is directed. If it is intended for legal person, please clarify terms of contract." This single question removes presumption without conflict.

The second common presumption is that silence means guilt. System assumes that failure to reply equals acceptance of claim. To defeat this, you act first. You send notice before accusation matures. Each early letter breaks expectation of silence. Law respects those who act promptly and in peace. By creating record of communication, you show awareness and responsibility.

Third presumption concerns jurisdiction. Institutions act as if their rules apply to all without question. You do not reject authority aggressively; you request proof of jurisdiction. You write, "Please confirm whether your authority extends to living man acting in private capacity." This question forces examination of foundation. It cannot be ignored without consequence. Silence becomes confession that no lawful authority exists beyond voluntary consent.

Fourth presumption involves debt. Councils and banks presume signature equals liability. They treat promise as payment. To correct, you ask for proof of loss. "Please provide evidence that debt claimed represents actual value lent by you and not created through accounting entry." When no proof comes, record stands. Silence becomes proof of absence of loss.

These examples show pattern. You do not argue. You ask questions that expose missing proof. Each unanswered question weakens illusion. Each notice served replaces assumption with evidence of inquiry. Law values those who seek understanding.

Keep list of presumptions you encounter and note how each was challenged. Over time, you will see repetition. The same few assumptions sustain entire system. Once exposed, they lose strength. Knowledge replaces fear. You realise that power of authority depends entirely on ignorance of people.

To preserve peace, avoid turning discovery into crusade. The goal is not to prove others wrong but to live truthfully. Correcting presumption is act of education, not rebellion. Each letter teaches both sender and receiver. When written in peace, even officials learn quietly. Many have never questioned foundation of their work. Your calm inquiry plants seed of awareness.

Patience remains essential. Bureaucracy moves slowly. Expect silence and delay. Time strengthens proof. Every day without reply confirms acceptance of your question as truth. Keep record tidy and wait. Rushing weakens process. Honour grows through endurance.

Understanding presumption also transforms personal perception. You begin to see assumptions everywhere, not only in law. Advertisements presume desire. News presumes fear. Social norms presume obedience. When awareness grows, illusion loses hold. Freedom is not escape from system but release from false belief.

Proof appears through observation. Look around at how often authority changes when questioned calmly. The clerk who once spoke harshly becomes polite after reading your letter. The agency that once threatened now apologises for delay. These small shifts are evidence that truth reshapes reality quietly.

Some presumptions are internal habits of mind. Many assume they are small, powerless, or unworthy of respect. These inner assumptions mirror external ones. When you write first notice, you confront both. Each act of honour breaks not only legal fiction but psychological conditioning. Confidence in law grows alongside confidence in self.

To maintain integrity of proof, continue acting with honesty. Never claim knowledge you do not possess. If unsure of legal concept, admit it. The one who seeks learning stands higher than one who pretends mastery. The record built on honesty cannot be destroyed.

Silence as proof may appear strange at first. Yet silence operates as law because it represents completion. When notice remains unanswered beyond time allowed, issue notice of default confirming matter settled. Write, "As no reply has been received within stated period, all statements within original notice are accepted as true and correct." This closes process with dignity. Law always requires conclusion.

Be careful not to misuse this principle. Silence becomes proof only after fair opportunity for reply. Setting impossible deadlines or confusing conditions turns peace into trap. The measure of honour lies in fairness extended to others. The system may abuse presumption; you must not. Truth needs no deceit.

Presumption also ends where witness begins. When others see your process and confirm honesty, illusion fades faster. Collective awareness replaces isolated struggle. Communities built on mutual respect weaken control of fiction. Each living man or woman becomes witness of truth for another.

Proof does not shout; it simply exists. When record is clear, even enemy recognises it. Officials may not admit openly, but their actions reveal respect. Letters cease, threats soften, tone changes. Proof needs no audience. Its presence alters energy around it.

You will reach point where presumption no longer frightens you. Every demand becomes invitation to dialogue. Every claim becomes chance to ask question. Fear dissolves because you understand mechanism behind illusion. Knowledge restores calm. The once intimidating letter becomes paper seeking answer. You reply in peace and carry on with life.

The greatest proof of all is your transformation. The system thrives on confusion. The man who remains clear proves that clarity exists. His peace is evidence that law and conscience can live together. No affidavit can match power of calm presence that radiates truth.

The chapter ends with simple realisation: presumption is shadow; proof is light. Shadows disappear when light appears. You are source of that light. The record you keep reflects it outward into world. Each notice written in honour, each silence recorded in patience, each truth spoken in peace—these form proof that freedom still lives wherever conscience remains awake.

The next chapter will bring all principles together. It will show how the living record becomes expression of natural law itself, demonstrating that every man and woman carries ability to create justice through written truth and peaceful action.

Chapter 12: Living Record, Living Law

Law without life is machinery. Life without law is chaos. The two must walk together if peace is to endure. The written record unites them. It transforms silent conscience into visible form. Each notice, declaration, and affidavit breathes life into principle. When you write truthfully and act honourably, law becomes living expression of your being. This is what it means to live under law of truth rather than law of control.

Living law is not invention of men. It is reflection of natural order that governs everything. The sun rises without decree, rivers flow without permission, and seed grows without contract. Harmony arises when actions follow natural rhythm. Human law was meant to mirror this pattern, to preserve fairness, and prevent harm. Yet in time, systems replaced principle with procedure. Paper replaced conscience. The living man or woman who builds private record restores balance by returning law to life.

The living record begins as simple letter written in good faith. It becomes living law when intention behind it aligns with truth. A paper filled with fear has no breath; a paper written in peace lives. The difference lies not in ink but in spirit. When you sign with clear conscience, your word carries authority of life itself. No statute can overrule that. The living word transcends artificial rule because it springs from same source that created justice.

Living record reminds world that law is service, not weapon. Councils, agencies, and courts exist to maintain harmony, not to enslave. Their legitimacy depends on honour. When they act without it, their authority fades. A single man or woman living in truth can expose imbalance of entire institution. Not through rebellion but through example. The record stands as mirror reflecting conscience of both writer and reader.

Every letter you write in peace adds pulse to body of living law. Each document joins chain of truth connecting generations. Future readers may find your words and see pattern of awareness growing through time. They will know freedom was never lost, only forgotten. The archive of honour preserves memory of liberty for those who come after.

Living law demands responsibility. You cannot hide behind ignorance once you understand truth. Knowledge brings duty to act wisely. Each notice written carries consequence. It shapes relationships and teaches others how to respond. The living being who writes in anger creates confusion. The one who writes in peace restores balance. Therefore, every word must pass through gate of conscience before reaching page.

This way of life transforms perception of justice. You begin to see law not as system outside yourself but as reflection within. Wrongdoing becomes imbalance seeking correction, not enemy to destroy. Forgiveness becomes part of lawful process because it restores harmony faster than punishment. The man who forgives does not surrender truth; he completes it.

The living record also changes how you see authority. You no longer fear officials because you recognise them as people performing tasks within belief system. You address them as equals, neither above nor below. Honour bridges difference. When you treat every officer, clerk, or judge with respect, you remind them of humanity beneath uniform. Many rediscover their own conscience through that exchange.

Living law cannot be codified because it moves with heart. It does not depend on memorising rules but on understanding principle behind them. Cause no harm, speak truth, keep faith, and act in peace. These few maxims guide every situation. When confused, return to them. They will reveal correct path without need for legislation.

The living record proves that justice can exist without punishment. Resolution through communication replaces revenge through control. When two men exchange notices in good faith, they settle matter through reason, not fear. This is essence of living law: conversation guided by conscience.

To live under living law, you must remain student forever. Pride ends growth. The wise admit they know little and continue learning through each letter written and each silence endured. Life itself becomes teacher. Every challenge tests understanding of patience and honour. Failure becomes lesson; success becomes reminder of responsibility.

Living law rewards transparency. When you act in open truth, deception loses power. Secrets breed corruption. The man who hides nothing cannot be blackmailed. The woman who tells truth fears no court. Transparency turns record into shield stronger than metal.

Your archive of honour is temple of living law. It houses evidence of growth, forgiveness, and strength. Each folder is chapter of journey from confusion to clarity. When you read old letters, you see how far you have travelled. The paper once written in fear now appears gentle. The language once defensive now sounds serene. This reflection proves evolution of spirit.

Living law also unites community. When enough people keep private records in peace, society begins to shift. Officials start responding with courtesy, institutions act more carefully, and disputes reduce. Honour spreads silently through example. No protest required, no speeches needed. People notice difference between aggression and composure. They begin to imitate calmness. That imitation becomes reform.

The man or woman who embodies living law becomes guide without claiming title. Others approach seeking advice not because of authority but because of serenity they feel. True leadership emerges naturally from presence of peace. You teach by living, not by commanding.

The living record also heals. Many write first letters out of pain or injustice. Through process of honourable communication, pain transforms into understanding. You realise conflict was teacher showing where patience lacked. Writing becomes therapy. Each document replaces bitterness with balance. The act of correspondence becomes act of healing.

The living record therefore serves three purposes: protection, education, and transformation. It protects by creating evidence, educates by revealing principle, and transforms by aligning mind with conscience. Few systems offer such balance. Most rely on punishment and reward. Living law relies on awareness. It trusts that once truth is known, correction follows naturally.

The next section will explore culmination of all these lessons, showing how the archive of honour becomes not only shield for individual but light for community, proving that law written in peace can guide entire nation back to balance without conflict or fear.

Living law reveals its strength not through power but through peace. It does not shout, threaten, or demand. It whispers through order, patience, and truth. The man or woman who follows it discovers that justice does not depend on system but on clarity of conscience. The private record becomes reflection of that clarity, showing world that peace can exist even inside structure built on fear.

When record and life merge, there is no difference between document and deed. Every action becomes notice of intent, every silence becomes declaration of peace, and every promise becomes affidavit of truth. This state marks birth of living law within you. It is not new law but return to natural order forgotten by many.

The archive you built in private now carries pulse of truth into community. Friends begin to notice your calmness. They ask how you stay composed amid confusion. You show them letters, not to impress, but to illustrate principle. You explain that order arises from honesty, not authority. Some will understand immediately, others later, but all will feel difference. Peace is contagious.

Living record proves that justice can function without punishment. Dispute resolved through written honour creates understanding, not resentment. Both sides retain dignity. The one who was wrong sees fairness; the one who was right feels compassion. This outcome is true restoration of law. It transforms enemies into witnesses of truth.

Over time, living law dissolves fear of authority. When you understand that every institution exists because people consent, threat loses edge. You respect officers but no longer tremble before them. You see human being beneath uniform and speak directly to that humanity. This recognition ends illusion of hierarchy. Law returns to equality of conscience.

Living record teaches faith in process rather than outcome. You learn to trust that truth, once spoken, will reach correct destination. Whether letter receives reply or not no longer matters. You have fulfilled duty to conscience. That is completion. The rest unfolds naturally.

The more you live by these principles, the more unnecessary conflict becomes. You stop seeking victory because you already stand in peace. You stop fearing loss because nothing essential can be taken. The world continues its noise, yet within you quiet certainty grows. The archive on your shelf becomes symbol of inner stillness.

Living law also restores sense of gratitude. You begin to thank those who challenge you because they sharpen understanding. Each difficult letter or confrontation becomes tool of refinement. Without resistance, patience cannot grow. You see that even system you once opposed serves purpose. It forces you to remember truth. Gratitude transforms perception of enemy into teacher.

As awareness deepens, you recognise connection between law and nature. Both operate through cycles. Notice and reply mirror day and night. Silence after notice mirrors winter's rest before spring's renewal. The patient man who waits for reply acts like farmer trusting seasons. He knows fruit appears only when time is right. Living law follows same rhythm. Nothing forced survives; everything natural endures.

Eventually, you will realise that living law cannot be written fully. It is lived, not codified. The best record can only point toward it. Each letter serves as bridge between world of paper and world of conscience. The bridge must remain open. When people cling to forms, they lose spirit. The purpose of record is to remind you of life beyond it.

The archive you have built stands as monument of peace. It will outlast disputes that inspired it. Years from now, those who find it will feel energy of sincerity within pages. They will see handwriting, dates, stamps, and calm tone. They will understand that these papers were not weapons but prayers for truth. In that moment, they will glimpse living law.

You do not need title or office to uphold law. You uphold it each time you tell truth kindly, each time you respond to aggression with patience, each time you keep record with care. The authority of state pales beside authority of conscience. The world may not yet recognise this fully, but history moves in that direction. Systems that ignore truth eventually fall; those aligned with it endure.

Living law unites diversity. It respects differences while holding everyone accountable to same principles of honour and fairness. In such world, disputes resolve through conversation, not courts. Communities govern themselves through trust and record of agreements. Paper remains tool but no longer master.

To live under living law is to remember who you are. You are not fiction of registration but living being of thought and spirit. Your words carry power to heal, clarify, and protect. When written in peace, they join universal language of truth. That language needs no translation. Every heart understands it instinctively.

When last notice is sent, when last affidavit filed, peace becomes permanent. The external process ends because internal process is complete. You no longer write to prove truth; you live it. Your archive becomes silent companion, reminding you that freedom was never privilege granted by government but natural state of honest being.

The living law remains simple: speak truth, honour promises, harm no one, and record what matters. Live by these and no authority can disturb your peace. Law will follow you rather than you following law.

The journey that began with first letter ends not with final document but with transformation of heart. You become embodiment of what you once wrote. Your life itself becomes lawful record. Those who meet you feel balance without need for explanation. In your silence, they sense justice. In your words, they hear peace.

When that day arrives, your archive becomes inheritance for next generation. It will teach them that freedom is not rebellion but responsibility. It will show that justice born from honour cannot be destroyed. And it will whisper reminder that living law never dies because it lives wherever truth is written with courage and kept in peace.

Final Thoughts: The Archive of Peace

The journey through record and honour ends not in victory but in stillness. What began as search for remedy becomes discovery of peace. The living man or woman who has walked path of lawful awareness no longer seeks to fight authority or prove truth. They understand that truth never needed defence. It only needed witness. The archive they have built stands as quiet testimony that conscience, once awakened, is strongest form of law.

Each folder, each page, and each signature now carries more than evidence. It holds memory of transformation. When you look at the archive, you no longer see battle but dialogue. Every letter that once felt like defence now reads like step toward understanding. You see how tone softened over time, how language became clearer, and how patience replaced anger. The record shows growth of spirit through written word.

The archive of peace is not weapon or shield anymore. It is mirror of truth. It reflects what happens when man or woman acts from conscience rather than reaction. Each document captures moment when fear met clarity and dissolved. The paper bears marks of ink, yet what it holds is freedom. It reminds you that peace is not absence of conflict but mastery of response.

Those who walk this path discover that law is not enemy. Law is tool that reveals nature of self. Every notice and affidavit teaches discipline, precision, and respect. The structure of lawful communication trains mind to think fairly. It demands patience and rewards honesty. Over time, these habits extend beyond paper. They become way of living.

To reach state of peace requires acceptance. Not all questions receive answers. Not all officials acknowledge honour. Some matters remain unresolved in world's eyes but complete in conscience. You learn that justice is inner condition before it becomes outer event. The system may ignore truth, yet life itself responds differently. Opportunities appear, conflicts fade, relationships improve. Peace becomes law of daily existence.

The archive also teaches forgiveness. Many begin journey filled with resentment toward system. Through process of writing and waiting, resentment melts. You realise most people inside institutions act from ignorance, not malice. They follow instructions because they do not know alternative. The archive turns anger into compassion. It transforms idea of enemy into image of brother lost in confusion.

This understanding gives birth to wisdom. You stop trying to convert others. You live example quietly. The best teaching comes through calmness, not debate. The one who lives truth has no need to preach it. Others feel presence of order and ask questions naturally. You answer gently, guiding them toward their own discovery. This is how honour multiplies.

The archive of peace also restores faith in humanity. Each unanswered notice that remains in file is reminder that silence can serve truth. Every patient reply you sent shows strength of dignity. In world built on rush and argument, such patience is rare. It proves that higher law still lives in hearts of those who choose it.

In practical sense, the archive continues to serve. Should dispute ever arise, evidence stands ready. Yet you will notice that need for defence decreases. Life aligns itself with peace. Circumstances that once caused anxiety now unfold smoothly. People respond to tone you carry. The world becomes reflection of inner harmony.

To preserve archive properly, add final note at end of each folder. Write short reflection describing lesson learned from matter. These notes turn legal record into spiritual diary. They show next reader that law and conscience are not separate subjects but parts of one path. Your descendants may one day read them and understand what freedom truly means.

Freedom is not defiance; it is mastery of self. The man who controls anger, fear, and impatience is already free. No decree or statute can bind him. The archive of peace records this mastery. It shows how external actions reveal internal discipline. Each entry proves that order outside mirrors order within.

There is humility in finishing this journey. You see how little paper truly matters once peace arrives. The letters, though precious, were only tools to reach understanding. The real archive lives in heart. It cannot burn or decay. It travels wherever you go. Every thought, every word, every action becomes page of ongoing record written through life itself.

Still, keeping physical archive remains act of honour. It ensures that memory of lawful living survives in visible form. It reminds others that freedom is practical, not mystical. Anyone with pen, paper, and courage can live by conscience. You do not need permission to act with honour. You only need awareness of truth and willingness to follow it.

When others find your work, some will see philosophy, others will see law, but few will see both together. Only those ready to live truth will understand that archive is living bridge between worlds. It connects written word with living law, outer structure with inner peace. It proves that law is not property of rulers but expression of truth within every human heart.

You may wonder what comes after peace. The answer is service. Once you reach calmness, life invites you to help others find same. You do not lead them, you accompany them. You share examples, not commands. The archive becomes gift to humanity. Its pages tell story that freedom is possible when conscience replaces fear.

Every law in existence depends on written record. The world is shaped by those who write. When living men and women begin writing from conscience instead of control, entire civilisation changes. Councils, courts, and governments reform because language of truth seeps into foundation. The archive of peace is seed of that transformation. It may look like small collection of papers, yet within it rests potential of entire new era of lawful living.

When you close final folder and place it upon shelf, pause for moment of gratitude. Feel weight of years contained within. You are not same person who began journey. You are calmer, wiser, and freer. The archive is proof of that change. It is not treasure to guard but example to live.

If one day you choose to share it, do so with humility. Remove pride, keep truth. Present it as story of discovery, not doctrine. Let others see that peace is reachable through patience and integrity. Teach that record is reflection of living law, and that living law belongs to all.

The archive of peace stands as silent companion to mankind's oldest promise: that truth shall set you free. It reminds us that freedom is not achieved by rebellion but by understanding. The law was never enemy. It simply waited for life to return. The living record brings that life back.

So live peacefully, write truthfully, and keep record faithfully. Let each page, each signature, and each silence bear witness that honour still walks among men. When final paper fades and only memory remains, the law will still live through those who continue writing in peace.

Did you love *The Private Record: How to Build Lawful Evidence of Truth and Standing*? Then you should read *Cease the Decree: Ending Contracts in Peace*[1] by Roger Davies!

[2]

What if the highest law was already written within you?

Cease the Decree is a profound exploration of peace, honour, and conscience. It guides the reader through a complete transformation of understanding, from fear of authority to the calm confidence of self-governance. The message is not rebellion but remembrance. You are already lawful because you are alive.

Across twelve chapters and a closing reflection, Roger Davies leads you through a process of awakening. You learn how to communicate with clarity, respond without hostility, and live in harmony with the Law of the Living. Each principle builds upon the last, showing that true freedom does not come from defiance but from awareness.

---

1. https://books2read.com/u/bOvqyA
2. https://books2read.com/u/bOvqyA

This is not a book about loopholes or technicalities. It is a study of conscience as the foundation of peace. The author explains how to stand with honour in every situation, how to speak truth in written form, and how to use silence as evidence of strength. Through stories, examples, and reflections, you see how ordinary moments become lawful acts when guided by integrity.

You will explore:• How to turn conflict into communication through written peace• The role of silence as agreement or boundary• The difference between truth and belief in lawful conduct• The meaning of forgiveness as the highest expression of authority• The power of private record and personal responsibility• How the Law of the Living governs all human interaction

Cease the Decree reminds the reader that law is not a system of control but a reflection of conscience. Governments and institutions depend on compliance, but conscience depends on awareness. When you act in peace, you reveal a different kind of power — one that cannot be taken or transferred.

This book belongs to the *Sovereign Action Series*, a collection that teaches living freedom through personal integrity and self-respect. Each volume focuses on a different aspect of lawful living, offering practical guidance grounded in philosophy rather than protest.

Roger Davies writes with calm precision, offering not argument but understanding. His words speak directly to those who feel disillusioned by authority yet seek a peaceful way to stand in truth. The path described here is demanding but attainable. It asks for discipline, patience, and compassion — the real tools of liberty.

Cease the Decree is more than reading material. It is an invitation to live differently. It reminds you that law without life is empty, but life guided by honour becomes the highest law of all.

Also by Roger Davies

Adventures in Sovereignty: Growing Up Free

The Secret of the Hidden Name

Sovereign Action

Cease the Decree: Ending Contracts in Peace

Council Tax Nullity: How to Challenge Local Tax Demands through Honour and Law

The Private Record: How to Build Lawful Evidence of Truth and Standing

Sovereign Foundations: Liberty, Rights, Consent

The Constitution of One: How the Bill of Rights Protects the Sovereign Man & Woman

From Subjects to Sovereigns: Reclaiming the Spirit of 1776

Liberty by Consent: Reclaiming Freedom Through the Law of Consent

Standalone

The Commonwealth Corporation: How Australia Was Turned Into a Business

The Legal Fiction: The Greatest Trick Ever Played on Humanity

The Sovereign Path: Living Free Beyond the System

Common Law: The True Law of the Living

Freedom by Rebuttal: How to Say No and Stand Free

The Magna Carta: Why It Is Important to Sovereign Men and Women
The Trust Game: Hidden Estates and the Cestui Que Vie Act
Freedom by Notice: Winning with Paperwork
The Hidden Contracts: How Governments Enslave the People
The Law of the Living: Admiralty Shadows and the Path to Sovereignty
Standing as a Living Man or Woman in Canada: Reclaiming Freedom Beyond Statutes and Policy
Sovereign Stories for Children: 14 Parables of Freedom, Truth, and Honour
The Definitive Sovereign Handbook: Do No Harm, Cause No Loss, Commit No Fraud

About the Author

Roger Davies researches the crossroads of commerce, policy, and personal sovereignty. He writes for readers who sense there is more to the story, who are ready to replace fear with honour and paperwork with plain truth. When not writing, he helps men and women organise their records, challenge unfounded claims, and build communities grounded in mutual aid and responsibility.

www.ingramcontent.com/pod-product-compliance
Lightning Source LLC
LaVergne TN
LVHW100329210926
848480LV00003B/1292